LONESOME
COWBOY

By
J'Wayne "Mac" McArthur

Printed by Watkins Printing
Logan, Utah

For information, write"
J'Wayne "Mac" McArthur
2737 S Buckboard DR
Franklin, ID 83237

Author: J'Wayne "Mac" McArthur

ISBN: 978-1-60921-009-0

TABLE OF CONTENTS

ACKNOWLEDGMENTS

After I finished the manuscript for this book I asked Lyle McNeal to read it and give me his opinion. To my surprise he liked "Lonesome Cowboy" the best of my three novels. He encouraged me to get it in print.

I also want to thank Billie Emert for giving it a final edit for punctuation before going to the printers. It helped to have more than just an old cowboy putting the words down and getting the punctuation right. She also gave me a lot of encouragement.

Jenni Hatch has helped greatly with the word processing. She had done a good job deciphering my writing.

The Johnson sisters, Ja Nae and Jessica have produced the great pencil drawings. I appreciate their fine work.

INTRODUCTION

This book has been a work in progress for almost twenty years. I cowboyed on the George Jergeson ranch the summers of 1949 to 1953. Many of the activities came from my days working at all kinds of jobs on the ranch.

The section about the sheriff and judge was not related in any way to the law enforcement or judicial elements in Pinedale, Wyoming. A very old acquaintance, Henry Ruland, was a member of the Pinedale law enforcement about the time of this story. I don't want him or any others to take this story in any way but fiction.

Many of the events, however, did happen to me. As you read the book you will feel the realism.

I have known and worked with many young men who were or wanted to be a cowboy. I got to know their personalities and many deep down emotions. This book is a composite of a lot of people, both male and female. I hope you can see yourself or someone you know in the characters of the book. Many happy reads.

FOREWORD

As a long-time colleague and friend of the author of "Lonesome Cowboy", Mr. J'Wayne McArthur and being familiar with most of his writings, I thoroughly enjoyed reading this latest book. This is a story that not only comes with sincere and real-life experiences of "Mac", but also yours truly, "Doc". Over the decades "Mac" and I have shared many of our pre-academic ranching and cowboying experiences with nostalgia for the "good ol days" in the West and on the open range.

Although the story is about a bruised and busted cowboy, most people living in today's current world will find some commonality with the characters in this book. I've also traveled over most of the country within this story and "Mac's" descriptive skills of these areas of the West makes the reader mentally feel like being there. This story is a modern day "Oater" or "B-Western" that I remember back in the 40's and early 50's that were at the Saturday Matinee.

Despite the story's fictional persona, it's reality is surely for anyone who's cowboyed, buckarooed, rodeoed, or "rode for the brand." It's one of the best Western stories I've read since the passing of a notable author whom I knew, read and viewed many of his works, the late Louis L'Amour.

"Mac" has taken this very real-life type story and articulated as a 'pard' I know who has walked in his boots in many of life's experiences. The loneliness of being a ranch hand or rodeo rider is extremely and emotionally accurate. "Mac" and I share the common love of the openness of the Western range, the smell of freshly rained on sagebrush, along with the family cohesiveness of small Western towns that he shares in this outstanding story.

Having been a cowboy like "Mac" and involved in the cowboy culture most of my life, it's an endangered lifestyle that must be preserved because of the historic "Code of the West" and personal ethics one learns. "Mac" has written "Lonesome Cowboy" in the style of not only the famous western story teller Louis L'Amour but Larry McMurty and the very notable Zane Grey as well. My late grandfather, having been a wrangler for Buffalo Bill Cody's Congress of Rough Riders and Wild West Show, would have enjoyed "Mac's" writing skills with this chronicle.

I strongly recommend you read this story "Lonesome Cowboy" and place yourself in the saddle of this significant contribution to our Nation's love of the West and cowboys. Keep your hands on the reins of the pages of this great tale.

Dr. Lyle G. "Doc" McNeal, Carnegie Professor
Range Livestock Specialist
Animal, Dairy and Veterinary Science Department
Utah State University, Logan, Utah

CASEY

‿

"This year's cow cutting has drawn more contestants than ever before," sang out the announcer. "We have seen twenty-two cutters, so far, in this last go-round and we still have five more left in the afternoon competition. Next up is number twenty-three, Jim Case. Casey, as his friends know him, placed fifth in the first go-round and third in the second. He needs an eighty-seven to move into first place."

Casey moved past the two turn back men as his two and one-half minutes started. He moved to the back of the herd and slowly worked his way into the cattle. He didn't pick an animal out to cut but, instead, waited to see which one he would have the best position on as they separated. A big, black bally steer worked its way to the edge as Casey moved his horse, Little Doc, through the herd. As soon as Casey moved his leg against Doc's side to position him, Doc knew which steer he was going to take out and work. Doc moved like a ballerina under Casey. Casey had spent two years getting him this far and knew he was ready. The Denver National Western Show was one of the biggest shows in the West and Casey was really proud to be sitting so well in the standings.

Doc didn't do one thing wrong. He worked his first steer to a stand still, then Casey went back and picked out another one. They changed the cattle just before Casey started his cut, but he had watched these steers in the last go-round. He saw one that he recognized as a runner. The rest he couldn't remember too well so he just had to try to read the cattle and pick one that would work. If he picked a sour steer that had gotten away from someone else it might give him trouble. This time he could peel one off the outside, to save time. As he approached the herd, a black steer peeled off to go around him. Casey nudged Doc and he took over from there. This steer was not as easy to work as the first one. All he wanted to do was crowd Doc. The good little horse gave ground but would not let the steer around him. The steer made a dash for the fence to get around Doc. As the steer dove for the corner, Doc faded back and pinned him to the fence. That cost Casey points for using the fence as a crutch to turn the steer, but he didn't have any other alternative. That steer was just not going to stop and turn. Doc worked the steer for the remaining thirty seconds and was in a good position to quit that steer. Casey touched Doc's neck and stepped down. Loosening his cinch, he walked Doc back out to the other contestants.

As Casey was walking away, he heard the announcer say, "Well, that was a fine performance by a horse with a great heritage, but it just wasn't enough to put Casey on top. Casey received an eighty-two from the judge. That still puts him in third place if he doesn't get pushed lower by one of the next four contestants."

Casey wished he'd picked a slower steer that last cut, but that's the way it goes. Cutting wasn't all the horse. Casey just couldn't read cattle like some of the old timers, but he was still better than most. He had spent a lot of hours gathering

cattle for range brandings as well as sorting for shipping, but on the ranch it was quite different from cutting in an arena. On the ranch, the horse had to crowd the cattle more to push them out of the herd. As soon as they were outside the herd, the herd holders picked them up and moved them to where the cut was being held. The cutter then went back for another critter.

Cutting was one of the greatest of all ranch activities at the show, Casey thought. He also enjoyed roping because it used the skills of the ranch cowboy. He had tried all of the rough stock events, but they weren't for him. He could ride a bronc with the best of them, but he couldn't see the sense in spurring the horse to get more buck out of him. He broke lots of colts and always used quieter ways that helped to keep a colt from bucking. If the colt did buck, he always sat up and rode him out. He didn't mind other people riding rough stock because to each his own. He knew the rough stock of a good contractor had a better life than most horses owned by city folk.

The other four cutters had their turns. The highest score was a seventy-one so that left Casey in third place. He had earned sixty-four hundred dollars for his placing. That was more than he could have made working on the ranch.

In the evening rodeo there were more steer ropers than usual. He always used his calf horse for heeling and had teamed up with John Walker, a top header. Not well known at the big shows, Casey was happy to be able to team up with John. They roped their steer in 6.4 seconds and had finished fourth in the go- round. They picked up two thousand two hundred fifty dollars each for a share of the purse. The calf roping final round would come the next day.

After feeding his two horses, he drove over to the motel room he had rented. It was 1:30 a.m. and he had to rope in the next afternoon's rodeo performance. He showered and climbed into the nice clean sheets for a good night's sleep.

All night long, he could see that last steer he cut. His body jerked uncontrollably, in his sleep, as unconscious thoughts took him back to the arena. When he awoke he didn't feel like he had slept too well, but then he didn't remember being awake at all so he must have slept some.

After shaving, Casey picked out one of his bright colored western shirts and slipped it on. He liked to wear a scarf around his neck this time of year to keep his neck warm. Picking out a good match, he tied it around his neck. He grabbed his down-filled coat and Resistol hat with the Wyoming crease as he went out the door. Casey always dressed nicely, but never loud or gaudy. He liked to wear good Wrangler jeans and Tony Lama cowboy boots. These were a must for his wardrobe. He always wore a trophy belt buckle on a handmade belt with the name "Casey" carved in the back.

Casey was forty-five years old and a smaller statured man who was trim and neat. He stood five feet eight inches and weighed one hundred fifty pounds. His sandy hair was well kept and he was always clean shaven. His blue eyes were alert and quick to catch any movement around him. His legs were bowed from hours in the saddle and were a little on the short side, but that made for a long waist. An ample amount of hair stood out on his arms and chest. He always had a tan and was in good health, probably due to all the time he spent in open country.

Open country also meant living a few miles from the closest ranch. This left Casey alone a lot of the time as a child. He had a sister who was much older so they had little in common. She had been more interested in getting away from the ranch and moving to the city while he could have cared less about the city.

Casey had worked on the ranch like a hand since he had turned eleven years old. As a youth, he drove a team raking hay during the hay season. By the time he was fifteen, he had progressed to mowing hay. He also helped with the fencing. During July he peeled fence posts before they were treated. He rode colts in the evenings once they had been started. By the time he was fifteen he was taking in other people's horses.

His dog and the horse he was working with were his closest friends. He loved animals and was thankful for having them to grow up with, but they didn't take the place of friends.

Casey didn't have anyone to share his hopes and dreams with. His dog and horse had to listen to his problems, recognize his moods and feelings and react accordingly. He didn't know how single people got along living alone without even an animal to be their friend. He didn't know what he would have done growing up if he hadn't had animals.

Jumping into his pickup, he drove to the café a block down the street. A lot of the cowboys were staying in the motel right next door to the café and it looked like a few were up for breakfast early, too. Casey saw Bob and Dave who were a couple of the cutting contestants he knew. They motioned for him to come sit down. He pulled up an extra chair and sat down feeling really hungry.

"What will you have cowboy?" the waitress asked.

"Oh, give me some bacon and eggs with the eggs over easy," Casey replied.

"Well, how was your night Casey?" one of the cowboys asked.

"I cut cattle all night," Casey replied.

"That's how I was at first, but now it doesn't bother me

much unless we lose one. Then I catch hell from myself all night for that," said the cowboy.

Just then in walked a couple of bikers dressed in black leather coats, pants, and big square toed boots. They had red bandanas tied around their heads to complete their look. "Let's sit over here in the corner, Jake, so we don't have to smell the cows," one of them said.

That kind of talk didn't sit well with Casey, but he wasn't one to pick a fight so he didn't say anything. The talk turned to the calf roping standings and what time Casey had to beat in the final go-round.

"Hey, did you dudes clean your boots before you came in here?" the smaller biker chided. "Isn't the smell terrible in here?" he continued.

That was about enough. Casey turned around and said, "Look Mister, if you don't like the smell, why don't you go to another café. We don't appreciate you in this one."

The loud mouth biker stood up and walked toward Casey. Casey turned his chair halfway away from the table and sat still. The talk in the café had ceased and every eye was on Jake as he walked toward Casey. As he reached down to grab Casey's coat, Casey came up with a left to the stomach that took Jake right off his feet. Next was a right on the chin and then a left to the nose. Jake reeled back trying to catch his balance but fell in a heap between two tables. Casey waited for Jake to start getting to his feet, then let him have a right upper cut that straightened him out backwards on the floor.

Ox stood up like he was going to take Casey on next, but

the two cowboys at the table stood up also. Casey just stood his ground.

"Next time you want breakfast, either keep your mouth shut or go where you won't disturb any cowboys or you'll get cow shit all over you. You get my drift," Casey said. "Now get this monkey out of here and don't come back again."

Ox helped Jake up and guided him to the door. As they were going through the door, Jake yelled back, "I'll get my gang and we'll get you, you son-of-a-bitch!"

Casey jumped up from his chair. That was all that was needed for Ox to hurry Jake out of the café and onto their bikes.

"Sit down Casey and relax," one of the cowboys said.

"Well Bob, I'm sorry but I can only take so much from those kind of people. Then I get peeved. It isn't that they are bikers that bothers me; it's the attitude they exhibit."

"I can see that. I must say, you sure handled the biker, especially when he outweighed you by thirty or forty pounds. I didn't think you were big enough to take that big ass, Casey. Did you Dave?"

"I thought maybe Casey was going to get all our plows cleaned by those two apes," Dave replied. "Where did you learn to hit like that Casey?"

Casey's memory flashed back to his high school days. He had boxed on the varsity boxing team all four years and lettered each year. He had gone undefeated with only one draw in the four years.

Right after high school, he had volunteered for the Army.

He didn't like the artillery line unit he was put in so when he read on the bulletin board they would have boxing tryouts in two weeks, it interested him. He worked out every night until the tryouts and was picked for the division team. There were only twelve boxers on the team and Casey found the competition of a high caliber.

Casey hadn't been at the division headquarters very long before the coach and commanding officer rotated back to the States. They had told the colonel in charge that Casey could handle the coaching and run the sports unit until another officer was assigned.

That was a very challenging time in his life. He had learned a lot from his high school coach and the Army coach so he put together and ran a tough program which kept the boxers in shape. He was glad he didn't have to box anymore. He realized even the sparring was hard on the brain.

He had to manage the financial program as well. Buying tickets, and arranging games and fights, took a lot of his time. At least the men in the athletic company didn't have to stand guard, do KP or march around. They were like gladiators and no one bothered them.

Soon, an officer was put in charge of the athletic company. He was an ROTC second lieutenant and was afraid of a captain, let alone a colonel, so Casey still had to handle all the finances and communications with the upper echelon.

Yes, he knew how he learned to hit hard and fast.

Casey's coach in high school was an ex-Marine and a tough coach. He taught Casey to throw a punch with his body, not just his arm. Jabs could come from the arm, but a punch had to have body in it. When Casey threw a punch, he drove off with the foot on that side and carried his weight through to his fist. His aim was four inches farther than his opponent's face. In that way, he drove through the face instead of just reaching the face. These punches hurt and caused momentary disunity in his opponent; they also gave him time for follow-up punches which were fast and well placed.

In the Army, he also learned to be a gentleman, a manager of men, and how to take responsibility; but his real love was training horses. He liked the excitement of buying and selling horses. Making money at it was a real challenge and an art.

Casey remembered the colonel asking him to reenlist for another tour in the Army. He had a really good job, but there was no chance of that. His place was with the horses on the ranch and at the rodeos.

Quickly Casey's mind came back to the question being asked. Casey didn't want to go into all the detail so he said, "Well, my dad taught me to protect myself and told me to get in the first punch. He always said if you can't back your play, shut up. If you intend on backing it, then don't take the first punch because that one could rattle you enough to get you whipped."

"It sure looks like you learned well," Bob said.

"Lordy, I'd sure like to have a punch like that," Dave chided in.

"Well, let's eat some breakfast and get to the show," Casey said.

Casey found Little Doc and Latigo Leo waiting for

breakfast too. He got a couple of flakes of hay for each horse and poured them each a half gallon of grain. The water was a few stalls away so he grabbed the buckets and went to fill them.

"Hi! Casey," a cowboy at the water tap greeted him.

"Well Hi, Will. I haven't seen you here all week," Casey said.

"I just came to pick up my bull dogging horses. Craig Mortensen borrowed them on shares for the show. I couldn't make it. I've been laid up the last couple of months 'cause of a steer wreck up at Douglas. I'm just now getting around a little."

"Why that's too bad Will. I hope you're getting well enough so you can do what pleases you," Casey said.

"It's my knee. A big steer rolled over me and stepped right on it. My doc told me that was the end of my steer wrestling, but hell, what does he know about cowboys? If they weren't tough, they wouldn't be cowboys."

"I guess that's right, Will. I sure have seen some wrecks and most of the ol' boys came back the next show. Some in casts, but they don't let that stop them."

"I hear you almost got in a wreck today, too," Will said.

"Oh? When was that?" Casey asked.

"Down at the café during breakfast some of the boys were talking about not making you mad 'cause you hit too hard to tangle with," Will said.

"Why Will, that's the first fight I've been in for years. I don't like to fight and I don't look for them, but that guy came over and asked me to hit him so there wasn't much else I could do. If it had been you, you would have done the same thing."

"Not anymore," Will replied as he hobbled off.

Casey filled the buckets and watered the horses. He really thought a lot of his two geldings. Every horse he had ever owned had a hole in him somewhere, but these two had given him fewer problems and performed better than any horse he had ever had. It was the greatest feeling to Casey to have a horse under him that he had trained, a horse that responded to his every cue. It seemed like ol' Doc and Latigo didn't even need cues anymore. They knew just what he wanted. All the time he'd spent practicing and competing on them had taught his horses and him to work together.

After feeding, Casey walked around the Coliseum looking at the exhibits and the livestock. He always enjoyed the Denver Show because there were so many things to look at, and he saw a lot of the old cowboys he knew from Wyoming.

He bought a hot dog and a drink for dinner, then went down to get Latigo saddled and warmed up for the calf roping.

The afternoon performance started at 2:00 P.M. The calf roping would be right after the bareback bronc riding. There were about ten calf ropers at each performance. Casey would rope next. There would still be one more performance that evening before Casey would know how he placed.

"The next roper will be Jim Case. He needs a time of 9.3 seconds to take the lead in the calf roping," the announcer barked.

The calf was in the chute but it wouldn't keep its head turned forward. The chute man was standing over the calf, on the chute, trying to keep the calf headed. Casey watched the calf's head and when he saw the calf was in good position, he nodded and the gate man opened the gate. The calf shot out with a little help from an electric cattle prod. As Latigo reached the end of the barrier, the barrier string popped open in front of Latigo. By this time the horse was already at the front of the chute and gaining on the calf. Latigo moved to the right giving Casey a good shot and out went the rope. The loop settled on the calf's head with a nice figure eight out to the side, then Casey pitched his slack and dismounted as Latigo buried his tail in the ground.

Casey had twenty-eight feet to cover from Latigo to the calf and he did it in five long strides. Latigo had tipped the calf upside down when he stopped. The calf was just getting to his feet as Casey got to him. This wasn't a big calf. Casey reached over the calf, grabbed the calf's flank with his left hand, then grabbed the rope with the right. Being left-handed made it so he didn't have to get off the right side of his horse. This was faster for him. Casey then laid the calf down hard on his side. That took the rest of the fight out of the calf. Casey slipped the pigging string on the upper front leg, then he brought the back feet up, took two wraps and a hooey and threw his hands up in the air ending his time.

Walking back to Latigo, he knew he had a good time, but 9.3 was a lot to hope for. Casey patted Latigo on the neck as he stepped up on the horse and moved him ahead to give slack on the rope.

The judges signaled it was a legal tie. The announcer

21

said, "13.2 for Casey. That puts him in fourth place with the 12.3 and the 12.1 he had on his previous two head. Well, consistency is a really good trait, Casey."

That wasn't so bad Casey thought. He usually tied his calves in around 13 seconds. It sure wasn't an unlucky number because he had won a lot of smaller shows with that time. This was the big time and he was not the best there, by any means.

He rode Latigo back to the stall and unsaddled him. He had to wait for the last performance to find out his final placing and he couldn't get paid until tomorrow anyway, so he decided to stick around.

There sure were a lot of pretty girls in fancy, western clothes running around, but most of them were with somebody. He hated being alone, but his life was kind of like a song he had heard on the radio titled "Cowboys Are Always Alone Even With Someone They Love."

Casey had had a few girlfriends, but he had only given his heart to one of them and that hadn't worked out. By not getting too serious, he didn't have to take the chance of getting hurt. He hadn't been able to find another woman who wanted what he did out of life. He wasn't sure he knew what kind of woman he wanted for life, but when she came along he would know it.

After the show, he walked out to the parking lot where he had left his pickup. As he walked around the fender, he heard a voice he recognized.

"Hey, cow shit stomper, we've got some unfinished business."

Casey looked around and saw Jake, Ox and two more of their cronies.

"Well, it looks like you got the rest of your gang to do your fighting, didn't you? I've heard this is the chickens' way of fighting. Did you bring your chains and pipes?" Casey prodded.

Casey couldn't see any where to run. There was no one in sight to help him. Maybe if he made them act foolish, he might have some kind of chance, but he sure didn't see much of one.

They were coming in fast. With one vault, Casey was up in the bed of the truck. He had an old shovel handle in the back of the truck but had never had any cause to use it before. He ducked down as a chain flew over his head. Casey grabbed the shovel handle with both hands.

Ox was just coming over the tailgate as the handle came up along side his head. He went down with a dead thud. Casey felt a chain wrap around his back straightening him up with pain. He had to keep swinging. He felt the handle hit another of the gang members and heard him yell with pain.

"My arm, it's broke! Kill that son-of-a-bitch," the biker yelled.

Casey looked around to see Jake standing on the running board of the truck, trying to get into the truck bed. Casey swung and caught him on the side of the head, slamming it into the cab. Blood was all over Jake's head as he slipped to the ground.

Blackness settled over Casey as a lead pipe hit his skull. He didn't feel the next two blows, which broke his arm and ribs.

Will had heard the commotion as he was getting into his truck to go home. He grabbed a tire iron and hobbled over just in time to see a guy hitting Casey with a pipe. Will walked up quietly and hit the biker in the legs. As the biker's body was draped over the bed of the truck, Will delivered a blow to his head that stopped him. Will walked around behind the truck where he heard some moaning. He saw the biker with the broken arm.

"Don't hit me. I'm hurt really bad. Please get me a doctor. Please don't hit me," said the biker with the broken arm.

Will stopped short of braining him too.

"Dave, Bob, come over here quick. Casey's been hurt," Will hollered.

One look at Casey and Bob ran for a phone to call the police and an ambulance.

It took more than fifteen minutes to get the ambulance there. Dave and Will covered Casey up and made him as warm as they could, but he hadn't moved or said a word. They could see he was hurt badly. They didn't want to move him until the medics came.

The police arrested the four bikers. Three of them were unconscious and didn't know about it at the time. They were all hauled to the hospital to get medical attention. Casey had made a mess of three of them and Will didn't go easy on the fourth. That biker had a shattered knee and a fractured skull.

It was three days before Casey started regaining

consciousness. By then, his arm had been set in a cast and his ribs were wrapped. He had to have a patch of hair removed on his head and stitches put in his scalp.

As Casey started coming around in the ICU, a cute little nurse was talking to him. As soon as he started responding, she left the room for the doctor.

The doctor came back and checked Casey's vitals. It was hard for Casey to stay with it. He kept coming in and out of consciousness.

"How are you feeling, Mr. Case?" the doctor asked.

"I'm not sure. I can't feel a whole lot right now," Casey responded. "How did I get here?"

"Do you remember the fight you were in with the bikers?" the doctor asked.

Casey drifted off into a deep sleep.

"Move Mr. Case to a regular room now. I think he will be okay. His vital signs are good and he appears to be a tough fighter for life," the doctor instructed the nurse.

When Casey came to, he looked around the room and saw someone in the bed next to him. The man's leg was in a cast all the way to the hip and was strung up on ropes. Casey looked down as his eyes were clearing and saw the cast on his arm. As he moved his arm, it fell back against his side. He moaned with pain. His back was sore. Then he remembered something hitting him. He was in pain, but before he could figure things out he drifted off to sleep again.

C H A P T E R   2

KIM

___

At 6:00AM, Samantha started making her rounds. Soon, she came to the room where Kim Randall and Jim Case were confined. It sure was a coincidence, she thought, that these two would end up in the same room in a Denver hospital.

As she looked at each of them, she could see the sun and wind-tanned hands and faces that came with ranch work. Kim was dark complected with a black moustache and a full head of black hair. He was a larger man than Jim Case. Kim, she thought, would stand five foot ten or eleven, but then she hadn't seen him standing up yet. Mr. Case was older and quite a bit smaller. He looked like he would not stand more than five feet eight inches at the most and didn't weigh over one hundred fifty pounds with his clothes on. He had a ruddy complexion with short, sandy hair. They both had blue eyes and she was sure the two men had a lot more in common.

She had been drawn quite close to Kim, even though she didn't want to let herself get involved emotionally with any patient. He was so fun to talk with. She knew she had nothing in common with him, but he needed someone to help him through these tough lonely days.

Going to Kim first, she picked up his hand and stuck a thermometer into his mouth just as he was about to say something.

"Good morning Kim. You have a roommate now. Won't

that be nice?" Samantha said.

Kim tried to mumble something but couldn't talk without dropping the thermometer out of his mouth so he stayed silent.

Finally, Samantha took it out of his mouth and read it. Then she put it in the 'used' container.

"What happened to him, Sam?" Kim questioned.

"Well, it seems as though four members of a bike gang took him on and they lost. They're all in the jail ward with some bad fractures. One of them hit him from behind with a pipe, fracturing his skull. They also broke his arm and ribs. He took care of three of them before they got him," Samantha said.

"Where was he to get in a mess like that anyway?" Kim asked.

"He was in the same place you were when you got hurt. He's a contestant at the show, too. He was just going out to get in his truck when they hit him," Samantha reported.

"Well, I hope he hasn't gone through as much as I have in this hospital," Kim said.

"He doesn't know what he's been through. He had only woken up once since he came into the ICU. At least he hasn't had any pain, but I'll bet he'll be wanting a shot when he does wake up. He started to wake up last night but then drifted off again. We're hoping he'll regain consciousness soon."

Kim glanced over as Casey moved his right hand with the cast on it and heard him groan as it came back against his ribs.

"Looks like he's coming around a little now, Sam."

Samantha walked over, took Casey's hand and checked his pulse. While she was holding his wrist, Casey looked up into her beautiful blue-gray eyes and tried to focus. Her beauty came to him and the first thought he had was Am I in heaven? She sure looked like an angel. Finally, his head cleared a little.

"Where am I? What happened? How did I get here?" he asked.

"You're in the Denver Memorial Hospital. You've been in a fight and the ambulance brought you here," she answered.

"How long have I been here?" Casey asked.

"About three days in the Intensive Care Unit," she told him.

"Three days! What about my horses? They were at the Coliseum," he questioned.

"A man came by the morning after they brought you in and left this note for you," Samantha said.

She opened the note for him, but his eyes still weren't focusing too well.

"Would you read it to me? I can't see the words yet," he said.

"It says:

Casey,

I had to leave for home, but I got Dave to drive your truck and trailer and haul your horses home for you. Bob is going to pick him up at the ranch. They said it wouldn't be much out of their way.

The Doc said you would be laid up in the hospital for a while and I knew you would want the horses taken care of, no matter what.

Hope you wake up and can read this. I wish I had gotten there sooner to help you, but you just about had them all whipped. Get better so you can go home soon.

Best of Luck,

Will

"At least the horses didn't have to go hungry because of me," Casey said.

"I'll bet it's nice to have friends like that," she said.

Kim broke in with, "I wouldn't know, I've never had one like that. My friend did this to me, wrecked my truck, and left with hardly a goodbye. Didn't she, Sam?"

Samantha grinned at Casey and turned to Kim, "Yes, I guess you could say that's about what she did, cowboy."

All at once, the pain in Casey's head started pounding and it almost made him pass out again. "Nurse, can I get something for a headache? My head feels like it's gonna explode. My chest hurts when I breathe, too," Casey said.

"I'll see if the doctor left any instructions for your medication," she said, then left the room.

"It took me nigh on to five hours to get some pain pills for my leg," Kim helpfully announced.

Without saying anything, Casey shut his eyes and tried to think the pain away. He drifted back in thought to the ranch in Pinedale, Wyoming, and the colts he still had to finish training. If only he could get out of here and back to the ranch, everything would be okay. He always felt safe and comfortable working with the horses.

Samantha returned with a syringe in one hand and her clipboard in the other.

"Turn over a little so I can hit your hip," she said.

He could hardly move, since he had an I.V. in one arm and a cast on the other. His ribs were really starting to pain just breathing, let alone moving.

"That's good, I can reach you there." With that, she jabbed the needle in. It stung a little as the morphine was forced into his hip.

Within fifteen minutes, the shot had taken the edge off the pain. He felt his face and realized he had four days' worth of growth.

When Samantha returned, Casey asked if he could get a shave because it was really uncomfortable with all that stubble.

"I'll see what I can do, Mr. Case," she replied.

"How come you call him Mr. Case and me Cowboy?" Kim asked, a little irritated.

"Well, I guess it's because he doesn't come on like a wild stallion. It's just good you're tied to that bed or I wouldn't even come in here. At least, Mr. Case hasn't had his hands coming at me from every direction," she replied.

"Well, Sam, you just wait 'til he gets that needle out of his arm and see if he ain't as interested as I am." Turning to Casey he said, "I've been trying to get Sam here to give me some sympathy, but all she gives me are pills."

Casey looked down and realized he was in a white hospital gown. He smelled slightly disinfected. "I suppose I've had a bath, too?" Casey asked.

"If you're like me, you hadn't changed your underwear either. Ma told me there'd be days like that, but you never think it'll happen to you. Ain't that right mister?" Kim said.

Casey remembered showering before he went to bed the night before, or was it four nights before. His head was still a little bit fuzzy, but things were fitting together.

"My name's Jim Case, but my friends call me Casey," he said.

"I'm Samantha Drew, Mr. Casey and this here lazy cowboy is Kim Randall from Spanish Fork, Utah," she said. "We would like to be your friends because it gets kinda lonely in here."

Before long, the doctor came by and checked Casey's eyes and looked at his ribs.

"That was sure a beating you took from that pipe and chain, Mr. Case. You're lucky it didn't kill you, but then you still came out of it better than the bikers. The one with the broken arm was transferred to the jail, but the other two you hit are still here. One of them hasn't regained consciousness yet. The one your friend hit didn't make it. He won't be using a lead pipe on anyone else, that's for sure. The police didn't hold your friend. They said it was self defense."

"How soon can I get out of here? I need to get back to the ranch," Casey said.

"Oh, it'll be a week or more before you'll be up and around with that punctured lung and the broken ribs. We put you back together, but you must take it easy or you'll rip things apart. You should take it really easy with that skull fracture, too. You'll need medication for the pain for a few days anyway." With that, the doctor left the room and shut the door.

"Well, Casey, it looks like we're going to be roommates for a while. I'm going to get out in a week or so, too. If you need a ride, we could use my outfit to get home. I've got to find it first, though. My girlfriend wrecked it and the police had it impounded," Kim said.

"I don't know what I'm doing right now," Casey said. "We can talk more about it when the time gets closer."

Kim pushed the button for the nurse and within a few minutes Samantha entered.

"Sam do you think you could help me? I need to find out where my truck is so the insurance company can get it fixed for me. I'll need a way out of this town."

"You can't drive with that cast on, silly," Samantha instructed.

"No, but Casey has two good legs and one good arm and I have two good arms and one good leg, so between us we have a man and a half. That ought to be enough to herd that truck and trailer down the road."

"I'll call the police station and see if I can locate it. Give me your insurance card and I'll try to find a body shop to repair it."

"It's in my wallet in my pants, Sam. You're sure a good kid to help me out like this."

Things were moving a little fast for Casey. He had just

woken up and already he had a guy wanting to be his partner. He remembered back to the years working with Scott Rinebow. They had been partners. A partner was something like a brother. You're kin to him, but not his dad and mother. He liked having Scott for a partner. It was a bond most people could never understand. A partner is someone who helps with work that has to be done. He shares the fun as well as the work. No one could be as good of a partner as Scott, but then he got hitched and that ended the partnership.

Time would tell whether Kim and he could be partners or even friends. He figured it wouldn't hurt to work together to get back home, no matter what.

The days drug on that week. The food was poor and the only thing that made it bearable for Casey was Samantha. She would talk to Casey and Kim and kid with them, but she stayed out of Kim's reach.

The needle came out of Casey's arm and he was able to move around a lot better. Samantha didn't stay away from him. She would rub his back while putting salve on the cuts twice a day. She liked to talk to him a lot and he liked the conversation, too. It would have been so easy for Casey to fall for her, but he figured she was not the kind of gal who could ride and rope or turn back cattle for him. He just wasn't about to let himself be tied down to some city gal that expected him to go to work at eight and come home at five each day. That just wasn't his way of life. That would kill him quicker than getting beat with a lead pipe.

Kim was always talking about the girls he had known. Casey figured Kim had lived with at least half a dozen and shacked up with three or four dozen more. His idea of a woman and what she was for was completely different from Casey's.

Casey remembered the old foreman on the Quarter Circle O telling him how to pick a woman. He said you picked a woman just like you would pick a horse. You wanted one with size and strong bones, to be able to do the work, and she should have wide hips, a full rump and be well V'ed up in the chest.

That was well and good if all you wanted her for was to raise kids and do chores, but Casey wasn't looking for that kind of a woman. He wanted a girl who was smaller with more refined bones and a slender profile. She didn't even need to have wide hips or a full rump. He liked them trim with no wasted flesh. As for being V'ed up in the chest, any more than a handful was surplus as far as he could see.

One thing he did like was light blue eyes. Eyes were the windows of the soul and if you looked deeply into them, you could read the inner most secrets. That's why he kept the shades pulled on his blue eyes most of the time. You couldn't have just anyone reading your secrets.

Casey could look deep into Samantha's eyes and read her feelings. She was very friendly and loving. She was the kind who most likely ended up on the wrong end of a love affair.

Kim couldn't read Sam's secrets, but he wanted to give her some more to store away. Kim was a very open person. When he wanted something, he just asked for it. He was a good-looking guy and easy to like, so he most likely could find a woman who was lonely and needed love. It didn't mean much to him as long as he got what he wanted. All a woman had to be was half good looking and hungry for love.

Samantha could see these two cowboys had different values, but she was lonesome and had feelings for both of them. The feelings were completely different. She found Kim excited the girl in her and she wanted to let him get hold of her. Casey excited the woman in her and she could feel the warm feelings he created inside her.

By Friday both Kim and Casey had been up with some help and had tried to walk around. They were both very shaky from their down time. Kim required crutches. Saturday was a little better and the doctor told them they could both leave the hospital the next Monday at noon.

They were two happy cowboys just waiting to get out of that hospital. Casey had called home for the second time and knew everything was going well. His dad had hired on an extra man to work for him while he was rodeoing so he hadn't put anyone out.

Kim never called anyone so Casey assumed he didn't have anyone who worried about him.

"Well, Casey, it looks like we're going to get out of here after all. Do you feel like you can handle a stick shift truck with a trailer behind?" Kim asked.

"Oh, by Monday I'll be able to handle a semi as long as it has power steering," Casey returned.

Casey didn't know what he was going to do with Kim once they got to Pinedale. Casey could drive home, but neither of them could work. Casey decided he could use the transportation home and would figure out what to do with Kim when he got there.

CHAPTER 3

FAREWELL

Monday finally came. Kim and Casey were up, shaved, and packed early.

"Here are your keys, Kim," Samantha said as she came through the door.

Kim caught them in the air and said, "You got it from the shop for us?"

"Yes, I thought it would be easier than taking a cab clear over there," she said. "I don't know how to hook up a trailer or I would have done that for you, too."

"We'll get some help at the coliseum to hook up, Samantha. It was really sweet of you just to pick up the truck for us," Casey inserted.

"Why, I didn't know you could drive a stick shift, Sam," Kim quizzed.

"You don't know a lot about me, Cowboy. My daddy drove truck for a while and he taught me how to double clutch the big ones."

"Dammit Casey, I told you we should take her with us. She could handle the drivin' as well as the nursing," Kim said.

"The orderlies will wheel you down to get checked out. I'll bring the pickup around to the door," Samantha said. Then she grabbed the keys back from Kim and rushed out the door.

Casey knew he would miss Samantha and could tell she was sad to see them go. He was too soft inside to hurt a lady; and when one was hurting, he wanted to comfort her. This was one time he had to hold his composure. Samantha was having a hard enough time with this, without him showing his feelings.

Kim and Casey were wheeled down to the desk and signed their release forms. Then they were pushed to the entrance where Samantha was waiting.

"You guys look worn out already, and you have only been up a few hours. You need someone to take care of you and you know it," Samantha said.

"Oh, we'll be fine once we get in the truck Samantha," Casey insisted.

She picked up their gear and followed the wheel chairs to the entrance where the pick-up was parked.

"Wait until I set this stuff in the back of the truck and I will help you," Samantha said.

Casey got out of his wheel chair, walked to the truck, then held the passenger door open while Samantha wheeled Kim up to the truck. Kim had his arms around her shoulders holding her very tightly. Samantha could feel the warmth of his body and had so much emotion swelling inside her. She hated to let these two guys just walk out the door and out of her life. She thought back to what Casey had said and knew there was nothing for her here. As Kim made it to the truck door, he reached down with both arms to hold Samantha. That was just what she expected from him.

"I hate to let you two guys leave," she said.

Kim gave her a kiss and said, "Leaving is what cowboys do. You know that."

Casey came around the truck door and grabbed Kim's arm. "Samantha, lift up on his other arm while he slides onto the seat. Now slide back toward the center of the cab, Kim, so we can get this cast in," Casey said.

Kim did as he was told and was soon far out of reach of Samantha. Casey could see there were some feelings rising in Kim, too. It was time to get out of there.

Shutting the door, Casey turned to look at Samantha. "We both care for you more than you know. Thanks for all your care and attention. Good luck, beautiful lady."

Kim heard it all, but didn't have much to say. He waved and blew Samantha a kiss as Casey came around and climbed into the cab.

Turning the key, Casey started the engine. "Okay, put it in gear," he said to Kim.

Kim slipped the gearshift into second and they started to move forward. They both glanced back at Samantha and waved.

They rode in silence for a time. Casey had not looked at Kim since they left the hospital, but now he turned to meet Kim's glance and said, "You know, you broke that gal's heart."

"Me! You had more of a hold on her than I did, if you ask me," Kim came back.

"Okay, we both hurt her and we should both be whipped,"

Casey said.

"You can take your whipping if it will make you feel better, Casey, but I don't feel any need to be punished. Girls know guys are just feeding them a line and should take everything with a grain of salt. If they don't, it's their problem."

Casey knew that was mostly true and knew those kind of guys would always stay that way.

C H A P T E R   4

LEG BREAKING

With Kim shifting and Casey steering and running the foot controls, they were handling the truck quite well.

"Why are those people honking and pointing at us? They can't see our casts," Kim said.

Just then, a car pulled up and the guy hollered to them, "It looks really cozy in there."

"What's he talking about?" Kim asked.

"Well, I guess we do look a little queer cuddled up on this side of the truck," Casey informed him.

"Queer! You mean gay? Why I'll be damned! I may have been accused of a lot of things, but never accused of that," Kim said.

"I think when we get to the coliseum, you should turn around and lean against the door. I don't like the insinuations either," Casey said.

"Gay is the last thing I will ever be. I love the opposite sex way too much for that sick stuff," Kim said.

They soon arrived at the coliseum and pulled up in front of Kim's trailer.

"Put it in reverse and I will try to back up to it," Casey said.

One try and it looked like they were very close. A fellow walking by stopped and guided Casey right onto the trailer ball.

"Thanks Mister, we kinda needed the help," Casey said.

"Oh! Do you have a hard time backing up to a trailer too?" he asked.

"No, we are a little disabled. Between the two of us, there is almost one full man," Casey said as he opened the door and stepped out.

"What the hell happened to you two guys?" the helper said.

"Well, that's a long story, but we could use a little help

hooking up and shifting my friend's position," Casey said.

"Sure, I'll lend you a hand. By the way, ain't you the guy that put those four bikers in the hospital?" he said.

"Yea, I guess I put three of them there, but my friend Will did the other one in," Casey returned.

"Boy, that must have been one hell of a fight. Everyone was talking about it the next day. You're going to have a reputation like those old gun fighters if you're not careful. They say you can hit like a man twice your size."

"Right now I couldn't kill a fly with a big swatter so, if you'll just help with the trailer, I would appreciate it," Casey said.

After the trailer was hooked up, Kim hollered at the helper. "Now you can open my door and help me out."

"Sure, partner, I'll be right there," he said as he walked around the truck.

"I have got to get turned around the other way. We can't ride like this any longer," Kim said.

The helper questioned, "Oh, why is that? Your buddy got B.O.?"

"No, we just can't have people think we're that friendly," Kim came back.

"They think you're gay, huh," the helper said.

"Gay! Have you ever seen a real cowboy that was gay? I'm not talking about those midnight or urban cowboy types, I mean real live cowboys," Kim said.

"No, I really haven't," he said.

The thought of two gay cowboys turned Casey's stomach.

There was something about a cowboy that said, "I am a man. I was born of the open country where men are men and would have it no other way."

There may have been people who dressed Western that were gay, but they weren't men made of the experiences that make a cowboy. These men have the feeling down deep which sex they are and they are not about to feel any different.

Hobbling around the front of the truck on his crutches Kim came to the driver's door and leaned against the seat.

"Help me lift him up on the seat, will you?" Casey asked.

Soon Kim was up on the seat and sliding back to the passenger door. The cast now sat on the seat between him and Casey.

Casey shut the door and thanked their helper. Starting the truck he said, "Put it in gear," but Kim could not lean over enough to reach the shift knob. Reaching through with his left hand, Casey pulled the truck into gear. They were on their way to the highway heading north.

Casey knew it would be much easier once they got on the freeway. His ribs still hurt to bend so shifting was painful. He only had his cast to rest on the wheel while shifting. Kim wanted to talk so Casey just listened.

"I'll have to tell you how I got in the hospital now that I've heard about your escapades. It all started with the announcer saying 'Settling down on the big bull, Red Booger, is Kim Randall from Spanish Fork, Utah. This bull is one of the toughest bulls in the Jensen Brother's string. Only three cowboys made it to the whistle on him last year. Yes, folks, Red Booger has made a long list of rodeo celebrities eat dirt. This being the first

44

show of the year, let's see how this up and coming cowboy handles him, or gets handled.'"

"That's all I needed. Every bit of encouragement helped!" Kim said.

"Bobby Brown was at my side helping me down on the big bull. Bobby had been one of the three last year to make a score on Red Booger."

"'He'll jump straight for the ceiling when he comes out,' Bobby told me, as I climbed down into the chute. 'Just stay up against the hump as close as you can. Keep your chest out and don't let him catch you leaning back.' After taking the final wrap around my hand with the loose end of the bull rope, I pounded my fingers shut as best I could. Sliding up tight against my hand and sucking my legs in position, I said, 'Let's see him.'"

"As the gate opened, ol' Booger exploded up and out. I could hardly believe how high he jumped. Most bucking horses I had ridden got that sort of height in their jumps, but bulls usually stay closer to the ground."

"The momentum of the up and outward jump of ol' Booger sucked me back from my hand. The bull came down hard. My spine was compressed from my neck clean into my tail bone. Two more big twisting jumps to the left and then came what I hated most, the spin. I always seemed to get behind the spin. This time was no different. I was already loose so the spin just finished me off. I felt myself slipping out of the spin with each jump. The next instant I was flung through the air. The ground came up hard. Booger's big, broad head and two, high-set horns came right around like a street sweeper to clean up a pile of manure. I raised up just as Booger's head hit. My belly was now resting on the bridge of the big bull's nose. One toss of that massive head and I was airborne again, but this time when I landed, I sprang to my feet and took off running."

"One of the clowns had distracted the bull's attention so the danger was over. It was pure luck. The bull had given me a toss into the air instead of grinding me into the ground."

"I have been lucky rodeoing, only three broken ribs, a dislocated shoulder, and bruised pride. Over the four years I have been riding the rodeo circuit, I have had nothing that put me in the hospital before now," Kim said.

"Two more bull riders tried their skill, but both ended up on the ground before the whistle. That ended the Denver National Western Rodeo for me."

"I never was much for big cities and Denver is no exception. I grew up close to a small town in Utah where my father was the foreman of a ranch. Cowboying came second nature to me. I was tough enough to stand the bumps and gutsy enough to go looking for more at the next show. After placing second in the saddle broncs and fifth in the bareback, I didn't feel too bad about my unsuccessful attempt to ride ol' Booger," Kim said.

"January in Denver was getting to me. All I wanted to do was pack up my gear and head south to Arizona where it was warmer. There were a few small winter shows I planned on hitting before the spring shows get underway. I thought maybe I would have good luck in Arizona," Kim added.

"First, I had to find Sparrow. Susie May was her real name,

but I nick named her Sparrow because she was small and never stopped eating. She was my bunk mate and traveling companion."

"Finally, I spotted her red hair and tight, emerald green, western jumpsuit over in the stands. She had a couple of cowboys on each side. I knew she was in her glory. The one thing Susie May liked most was attention," Kim told Casey.

Casey could see his first impression of Kim wasn't far off.

Kim continued. "Susie's specialty on horseback was barrel racing, but that wasn't the redhead's best game. However, riding had sure helped keep her rear end firm. Besides a body, she had beauty splashed all over her face."

"Hey, Sparrow, I'll get my gear, then let's roll out of here," I shouted to her.

"She took her time telling the boys good-bye before heading down to the arena to meet me. Wherever she walked, she played to her audience and these cowboys knew they had just seen something. They didn't all have the same vision of what was inside that jumpsuit, but they all wanted to find out. Susie's wiggling hips didn't do anything to douse their desire."

"'Let's get something to eat before we leave town. I'm starved,' was Susie's greeting. I agreed. I didn't want to argue about food that night."

"As we walked across the arena, I thought how much nicer it would be driving my new Ford pickup down south than that gas-eating Jimmy I'd traded in. The stick shift had really made a difference in the gas mileage coming across Wyoming this trip. Besides, the two-tone paint job matched my trailer and that gave me pride in my outfit."

"When we first arrived at the stock show, I unhooked the trailer so the truck wouldn't be sticking out so far. There was a parking spot next to the trailer, so I parked the truck there with the back bumper next to the concrete foundation of the huge indoor arena. This was one outfit I didn't want all dinged up before it was broke in."

"I lowered the tailgate and hollered to Susie, 'As soon as I get our gear into the back, start the truck up and pull over to the trailer,' " I told Susie.

"Being small, Susie had a job climbing up into the new four-wheel drive truck's cab. She liked my old truck better because it was lower and easier to get into, and much easier to drive. The cold air was freezing her fingers so it was difficult to put the key into the ignition. She rested her foot on the gas pedal and turned the key. The truck shot back with the force of ten bulls. I saw it coming, but couldn't move fast enough to get clear. The lowered tailgate pinned my legs to the wall. The truck's engine killed in gear, with the tailgate tight against my legs. Susie May had forgotten to put in the clutch. Can you believe that, Casey?"

"Susie knew immediately what she had done. She was upset with herself for forgetting, but she was even more upset with me for buying a standard shift. She had tried to get me to buy the automatic, but I had to have the stick shift."

"Jumping out of the truck, Susie hollered, 'I told you to get the automatic, but you wouldn't listen. If you had, this wouldn't have happened. It's all your fault! You never listen to me, damn you!'"

"I couldn't make out much of anything she was saying. I was concentrating on pushing the truck ahead far enough to free my legs. I told her to put it in neutral. I got a couple of inches slack, and with my hands on the tailgate for support, I edged my way to the side of the truck."

"Susie was still hollering about something, but I couldn't make it out and I didn't really care. It was all I could do to keep from screaming with pain as I edged my way up the passenger's side of the pickup to the door. Opening the door, I pulled myself up against the seat; but I couldn't make the muscles in my thighs lift my legs."

"Come over here and help me get in," I hollered.

"'What would you do without me to do your little jobs? It's always 'do this or do that.' 'Who was your servant last year?' Susie complained as she walked around the front of the truck. 'You're not really hurt, are you? You just want some attention. It's the little boy in you coming out again,' she said."

"She grabbed my legs and started lifting and shoving."

"I hollered, Oh! Stop! Damn it, stop! My legs are painin' like hell so take it a little easy will you?" I gasped.

It finally dawned on Susie I might really be hurt. With more care, she helped me slide further in on the seat while holding my legs out straight. Once I was in far enough, she eased my legs to the floor. She could see the pain in my face and even acted sorry, but mostly I think she still felt it was my fault for buying that stick shift pickup. Can you imagine that?"

"'Now get in,' I said, 'and see if you can find the closest hospital. This time remember to put in the clutch, dummy!'"

"'But I don't know where the hospital is, honey,' Susie insisted."

"'Stop and ask at the first place we come to,' I told her."

"The first place just happened to be a drive-in. Susie pulled in and jumped down. She wasn't in much of a hurry, I thought, but all I could do was grit my teeth and hold tight to the seat. I could see my knuckles were white from trying to hold myself motionless. The inside of my cheek was hurting from biting it."

"After a few long minutes, Susie sauntered out of the drive-in and yelled, 'Would you like a drink and a sandwich?' Can you imagine that?"

"I rolled my window down and hollered back, 'get your butt over here and get me to the hospital, you bird brain!'"

"She vanished inside again and then came to the truck with a big frown on her face and a candy bar in her hand. Grumbling, she climbed back in, ground the gears, and headed the truck out of the drive-in."

"'Well, did you find out how to get to the hospital?' I asked."

"'They told me how, but you know I'm not too good at understanding directions. I always get lost,' she complained."

"'This is one time you damn well better not get lost or you can get lost for good!' I told her."

"We followed the hospital signs because she couldn't remember the instructions."

"Finally, the hospital was in sight. I had never liked the sight or smell of hospitals, but right then this one looked very good to me."

"Susie came around and helped me get my legs out. Then she helped support me while I hobbled into the Emergency Room."

"A chubby orderly in a tight, white jacket and pants that were four inches off the floor met us at the door and helped me to the table."

"'What's your problem, cowboy? You get hurt at the

rodeo,' he asked."

"Well, not quite, mister. My helpful friend here just tried to drive over me outside the arena, I explained."

"'Looks like she made it,' he said."

"What about something for the pain? I asked, trying not to grimace too much."

"'Oh, I can't give you anything until the doctor orders it,' the orderly informed me."

"Well, let's get that damn doctor down here 'cause it hurts like hell and it ain't getting any better, I told him."

"'Which doctor would you like?' asked the orderly."

"The closest one, you idiot. I don't know any of them. I'm from Utah and up until now I have had no need for a Denver doctor, I told him."

"'Okay, okay. Just lay back and try to relax while I locate one for you,' the orderly told me, and hurried out of the room."

"I hurt bad, but answered the questions Susie asked as she filled out the medical forms the Emergency Room clerk had asked her to complete."

"It seemed like an hour before the doctor finally showed up. When he did, he and Susie could hardly take their eyes off each other. Even I had to admit he was handsome, young, and mighty professional looking. His bright blue eyes seemed to be hypnotizing Susie as they exchanged smiles."

"Hey, doc, it's me that's hurtin'. She can wait, I told him."

"The doctor shifted his gaze to my leg and said, 'What happened, cowboy? Did you get thrown or stepped on?'"

"Hell no! Susie here tried to run over me with my own truck, I told him."

"'She what?' he said."

"She backed my truck into me against a wall and pinned my legs, and they hurt like hell, I replied. How about something for the pain? I asked."

"'In a minute, cowboy. First we must find out if anything is broken, but I can't examine your legs with your pants on. Take off your clothes and put this bed shirt on,' the doctor said as he tossed me a small, white bundle."

"'Would you like to step out here, young lady?' the doctor asked Susie. He and Susie started for the door. She was all body as she walked through the door in front of the doctor, and the doc was all eyes. I was too preoccupied to worry about that right then."

"Unbuckling my belt and unzipping my pants was not hard, but getting them off seemed impossible. After watching me struggle for a few minutes, the orderly offered to help. First he had to pull off my boots. The orderly started pulling on the boot as if it would come right off. Stop! Oh Stop! I shouted. You're painin' me something awful! Pull first on the heel and then the toe. Take it easy, I told him. I left my underwear on, but I sure wished I had changed that morning because, as my mother used to say, 'You never know when you may end up in the hospital'. Do you remember that, Casey?"

"Sitting up, I tried to figure out the bed shirt. It had three armholes. I knew I didn't have three arms so I was really stumped. The orderly finally took pity on me and explained the shirt wrapped around so one arm went through two of the holes."

"The pain in my legs was getting worse and I had been laying there for quite sometime."

"Where the hell is that doctor? I asked the orderly."

"'I saw the doctor and your young lady walking to the coffee shop,' he told me."

"Well, you go tell him I'm ready and waiting, and the pain isn't gettin' any lighter. Remind him, I'm first! I told the orderly."

"The doctor and Susie finally came back. I was more than a little upset by then.

The doctor could tell it too so he went right to work.

"'Can you bend your knees?' he asked."

"The knees weren't hit so they work fine. It's the thighs that got pinned. I can still put weight on my legs, but it hurts and the thigh muscles won't lift my legs anymore, I told him."

"'Oh, it's probably a bruise. They don't look like they're hurt bad. No swelling or discoloration,' the doctor told me."

"You ought to be on this side and you wouldn't say that, Doc. They hurt like hell and I could sure use a painkiller, I told him."

"'We'll just take some pictures of your legs and then we'll know just how bad they are. Can you walk down to x-ray or do you need a wheelchair?' he asked me. Wasn't that stupid, Casey?"

"I can walk, but I sure don't want to unless I have to, I told him."

"He told the orderly to get a wheelchair for me and take me down to x-ray where Janet would take pictures of both thighs."

"'Then we'll see if he needs a room,' the doctor said."

"The x-ray technician, Janet, had quite a build! I wasn't hurting too much to notice that. If her draftsman had been designing buildings, he would have been fired because his design was top heavy, but then it was anchored with an adequate bottom."

"'The doctor wants pictures of each thigh, Janet,' the orderly told her."

"She told the orderly to set my boots and clothes in the corner."

"She looked at my legs and said, 'Okay, cowboy, lie down on the table.'"

"How about some help! My legs ain't working the best, I told her."

"She came up beside me and I put my arm around her shoulders for support as I pulled myself up with the other hand. Finally, the table was about even with my rear end so I sat down."

"I jerked with the feel of the cold slab table. "What the hell did you do, refrigerate this slab? I asked her if everything in there was as cold as that table."

"'Only during working hours,' she replied. 'Now, turn over on your side facing the wall with your legs apart.'"

"Being a very modest man in public, I tried to get in the right position while shifting my gown as I moved. This isn't the easiest thing to do, you know, I said."

"She said, 'Oh, you're doing fine, cowboy. Don't worry, I've seen more men's bottoms than you have women's, I'll bet.'"

"I won't bet, but maybe later we can get together and compare, I replied."

"'Compare what?' she said. 'I've heard about you cowboys, and I think everything I've heard is true.'"

"By the way where is my pain pill? It doesn't look like you're going to give me anything to help me forget the pain." I said.

"I thought Janet would never get through taking pictures. She turned me on one side, then the other and then on my back. The table had warmed up and it was exciting to watch her work anyway."

"After some time, the doctor returned with Susie. Apparently she hadn't been lonely. They had probably been at the coffee shop eating again, I figured."

"Picking up the x-ray films, the doctor studied them for a few minutes and then turned to me."

"'You're a very lucky cowboy. Your left leg is broken, but the bones have not moved apart in any way, and the right one is just bone and muscle bruised. It should only take a few days of being completely immobile and you can be up walking around with a walking cast for six weeks. I could put the cast on now. There's hardly any swelling, but I'd rather wait a few days. We won't even have to put a heavy cast on your leg, just a walking cast to hold the bone in place.'"

"'How lucky can you be, Kim?' Susie inserted. 'Just think,

it could have really hurt you.'"

"Hurt me! Why the hell do you think I kept gritting my teeth? Did you think I was cracking nuts? I snapped. I still need some pain killers."

"'Well, you know what I mean, honey. Anyway, the doctor said you could probably go home after you get the cast on,' she told me."

"I told her, Gee, thanks for the help. All I need is more of your help and I'll have more need of an undertaker than a doctor. But then, what else could go wrong? I thought."

"'Now, honey, you know I didn't mean to hit you and you know you'll be better off in here. I'm really not much good as a nurse anyway,' she told me."

"By then I had gotten a pain pill and was feeling a little groggy, but not so much I forgot about my truck. Reluctantly, I told Susie she could drive the truck but to be sure to be careful. I didn't want it all dinged up."

"'Okay, let's get him a bed,' the doctor told the orderly."

"Where are you going to stay while I'm in here? I asked Susie."

"She searched for a good answer and then she said, 'Oh, I have an ol' schoolmate who moved to Denver. I can most likely stay with her. I'll be okay. You know me.'"

"Yeah, that's what worried me, but then she wasn't tied to me anyhow, I thought."

"'Oh, you don't have to worry, honey. I'll be in every day to see you,' she said."

"The doctor wasn't too fast, but he finally prepared the

paperwork and I was ready to go to a room. It seemed like I would never get to lie down and rest. It was now 3:00 a.m. It had been four hours since I was injured. That must have been a record for hospital speed, I figured."

"The orderly wheeled me down to the room and helped me get in bed. Susie followed along. It was almost morning by then."

"The orderly pulled out a diagram."

"I asked him what he was going to do now?"

"The orderly told me the doctor said I had to have a weight on my leg. He said he had only helped put one on before, but was sure it wouldn't be hard."

"How long is this going to take, the rest of the night?" I asked.

"The orderly departed, then returned with a box of pipes and ropes. The frame was attached to the foot and head of the bed. Then the ropes were strung. The apparatus was going up very fast."

"He asked Susie if she could help him put the weight on."

"'Sure, what do you want me to do?' she replied."

"When I lift the weight up, attach the rope from his foot and the one from the brace to the hook on top of the weight,' he said."

"As he lifted the weight, Susie slipped the rope from my foot onto the hook. She then took the rope from the frame to slip it on."

"'Okay, I've got it,' she told him."

"The orderly withdrew his hands. As he did, the weight hurtled toward my broken leg. As it hit, it jerked my leg from the rope that was attached. The frame rope had not been attached completely, letting the weight fall."

"I screamed as the broken leg took a swift blow right where the break was and got jerked all at the same time. The pain which shot through my body made me think the top of my head was going to blow off."

"I felt the bone snap this time. I knew my leg was completely broken now. It was as if I had no painkiller for I hurt worse than before."

"You damn fools! Get that doctor in here and quick! I screamed at the orderly."

"Susie ran down the hall in search of the doctor while the orderly tried to calm me down. I was twisting and turning with pain which didn't help the broken leg that was tied in a foot ramp on the bed."

"The orderly kept trying to reassure me I would be okay. I knew better, but I was getting as upset from the way things had happened as I was from the pain. I didn't have time or money to spend in a hospital, and the orderly wasn't making me feel any better."

"Susie and the doctor rushed into the room. The nurse behind them went around the bed, threw up my bed shirt and gave me a shot in the hip. That didn't make me any less upset."

"'Okay, cowboy, you're all right. Just settle down and we'll see what you've done,' the doctor said."

"What I've done! Why, that stupid femme and Susie almost killed me and you say, What I've done? The way it feels, they broke it good, I told him."

"The doctor felt the leg and sure enough, the bone was dislocated which made a big lump on my thigh. The pain shot had started to take hold, but it didn't help my state of mind."

"The doctor finally got my leg set, but now it was starting to swell. This time I would have to have the weights tied directly to my leg just below the knee with a metal pin through the leg, the doctor told me. Can you imagine how he was going to do that, Casey?"

"He called the nurse and she brought another syringe. The doctor deadened my leg from the hip down. Then he departed, returning shortly with a brace and bit. Making an incision in the skin just below the knee, he inserted the bit and began to drill. It was slow going and I could hear the bit grinding against the bone and see the bone chips fall from my leg."

"Now, riding bulls is one thing and I could psyche myself up for that, but this here drilling was something else. The drilling about made me sick. It wasn't the pain, but the thought of that damn doctor drilling a hole through my leg. On one side was the doctor drilling, and on the other the nurse securing my leg. Can you picture that?"

"Finally, the drilling was done and the pin was in place. The doctor rigged the weight, with the nurse's help and left Susie and me alone. It was 5:00 a.m. so Susie decided to sleep in the chair until morning."

"We both dropped off to sleep. We didn't have long to sleep. By 6:00 a.m. the nurses made their morning rounds."

"The shot had about worn off, and my leg reminded me of the time Susie smashed my fingers in the tailgate of the truck. The pulsating was about a hundred times greater. The pain from each beat felt like it was going to make my head explode. It hurt so badly I hardly noticed the way my ribs and other leg were aching."

"Into my room came a black-haired angel of mercy with a thermometer and blood pressure apparatus. This is when I met Samantha."

"'Looks like you're hog tied, cowboy. I shouldn't have any trouble handling you,' she joked as she inserted the thermometer in my mouth before I could say anything. She took my blood pressure and pulse while I was speechless, but not being able to talk didn't keep me from appreciating how her blue-gray eyes sparkled and how well her uniform fit. Her black hair flowed toward her waist."

"The angel told me 'It's time to get washed for breakfast. After breakfast, I'll be back to give you a bath. You smell like a horse,' she said, trying to help me forget how much I was hurting."

"While I washed my hands and face, I asked the nurse for something to help with the pain. She promised she would see what she could do."

"'It looks like you're in good hands, cowboy,' Susie said with a jealous note. 'I think I'll go find some sympathy, too.'"

"I said, Watch out for that young doctor. I'll bet he'll examine more than you bargain for, the way he looked at you."

"As Susie headed for the door, I hollered for her to take care of my truck. Without turning around, Susie said, 'I'll see you next time I'm here, whenever that is.'"

"I wasn't sure if she meant the next time she was in Denver or in the hospital. At any rate, I didn't really care after the trouble she had caused. But then, she had been a good bunkmate and I remembered she did have the keys to my truck.

"A nurse's aide soon brought my breakfast and rolled up the head of my bed so I could eat. She told me I had to wait an hour before I could have another shot. The nurse would be in as soon as it was time.

"Breakfast wasn't very good and I didn't feel much like eating right then. I tried to eat as much of it as I could so I could keep my strength up."

"I no sooner got my breakfast down when it started to come back up. Giving the buzzer a push, I tried to hold on until a nurse came. I waited and waited, trying not to think of it, but as it started crawling up my throat, I decided she would never make it in time. Leaning over, I strained to open the night stand drawer. I could see a wash basin and a spittoon pan, but they were too far back to reach. I had to get a little bit closer. Sliding my hips over just a bit more might do it. Now, to reach the pan, I thought."

"Crash!!"

"Down I went, head first for the floor. I put my hands

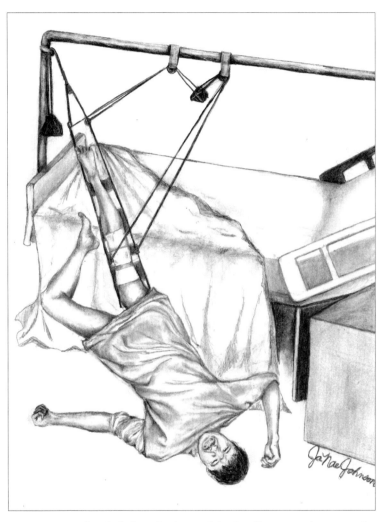

out to stop the fall, but before I hit the floor my leg caught me and there I hung from the pin in my leg. All I could do was scream. You'd have thought they didn't have a shortage of nurses after all, the way they came running. After the medical personnel had lifted me back into bed, I started vomiting convulsively. Besides dislodging the leg bone again, I was having other problems now. I had been on some good drunks, but this topped them all. Talk about dry heaves, I had them until they hurt worse than my broken leg. Then I passed out."

"Nurses and doctors were checking here, pushing there, and finally after I started convulsing and hyperventilating, they rushed me into the Intensive Care Unit. That was when the real torture began. They started putting fluids into each arm with needles as big as the ones I used on horses."

"The next few days were fuzzed by painkillers, but nothing could erase those damn needles in my arms. Just looking at them upset me. To make sure I wouldn't take them out, they had tied each of my arms to a board attached to the side of the bed. It was like being strapped down while a bull walked all over the top of me. So, besides hurting all over, one place as much as the other, I had to endure the indignities of being helpless. The frustration of being treated like a 'thing' really got to me. Finally, after I'd spent three days in Intensive Care, the same young doctor who'd started things in the Emergency Room stopped by to remove one of the needles."

"He said, 'Hello, how are you doing, Kim?'"

"What the hell are you guys trying to do, kill me? I said. You just about succeeded. All I came in here for was to have somebody check my leg. Next time I'll just lay in the back of my truck where it's safe and get better. I've had about all the hospital I can stand for one accident."

"The doctor told me I had had a close call. He said the second separation of my leg caused a blood clot and it started to move. It lodged in my lungs and I just about didn't need my boots and hat anymore. Once I was stabilized, they moved me back to my room. The doc told me they would take out the needle in my left arm. He told me that in about two more weeks he might be able to put a cast on my leg and let me start trying to navigate on my own again."

"I screamed, two more weeks! I can't survive two weeks in here! Already you've come closer to killing me than any bull or horse ever did. Just get my pants and let me out of here."

"'Nothing doing. You couldn't get to the door even if I let you try. You cowboys may think you're tough, at least you generally smell strong, but there are limits,' the doctor said."

"I thought for a minute. The comfortable horse and barn smells were gone. I smelled as clean as a bed sheet. Come to think of it, I did vaguely remember being sloshed with a washcloth. But the details of whom and when were as gone as my clothes."

"Soon after I was back in my room, Sam came around."

"She said, 'It's nice to see you feeling better, cowboy. We almost lost you over the Great Divide, you know. You cowboys must be almost as tough as you like to act, the way you fought for life. I suppose you know you're going to be hog tied for sometime yet, though.' She said, 'I will try to keep a close eye on you so you won't take any more acrobatic flips out of bed.'"

"'By the way, how do you feel now you are cleaned up? You weren't too cooperative to bathe, I heard. They thought you were going to break your leg again or the nurse's arm the first time they bathed you.'"

"'All I want is for you to keep clean and comfortable. We can't have you somehow starting to smell like a horse again,' she said."

"I told her, Now, wait a second, miss. A horse don't smell bad. In fact, most of the time I can hardly smell them."

"'That's the problem,' she said. 'You can't smell them because you both smell alike. You cowboys are all the same on that score, but I have to admit, you may be a special sort. There's certainly no doubt about your being a man . . . nor about how much you want to live.'"

"While she was bathing me, I was quizzing her about how I had acted while I was out. I knew I could be pretty ornery when I was drunk and since that was the way I had felt, I wondered just what had gone on. She told me I was no model patient, but then I was really sick, too. She said they overlooked all the names I called them and times I tried to kick them with my good leg while they were bathing me."

"She asked if the bath hadn't felt good after completing it."

"I told her, Yeah, it really did, and I'd sure like to pay you back in kind. I told her any time she needed help with her bath not to hesitate to ask".

"About then Susie walked through the door."

"'Isn't this the scene I left? Haven't you two been apart since I was here last,' she continued without being answered. She told me I was looking good. 'You probably didn't even miss me, did you?'"

"I told her, Well, to tell the truth, Sparrow, I didn't even know you hadn't been in."

"She said, 'That's gratitude, after all I've done for you, you big creep.' She said she was going to Arizona with a couple of the boys she met at the rodeo. She said she was leaving that day."

"Hey, wait a minute," I said. "You haven't heard the whole story yet. I've been . . . I tried to tell her when she broke in."

"'You've been what? Sick? I'll bet you've been sick. I'll bet you've been making out with little white pajamas.' With that she turned and strutted out of the room."

"I looked at Samantha and wondered what else could go wrong. The way I was trussed up there was nothing I could do to stop her, even if I wanted to."

"Just then Susie stuck her head back in the doorway and said, 'Oh, by the way, I wrecked your pickup. Here's the keys to what's left. The police had it towed off to some garage. They told me which one, but I can't remember the name.' Then she turned and vanished around the door."

"Can you believe that, Casey?" asked Kim.

"Despondently, I threw up the arm without the needle in it. Then turning to Samantha, I smiled and said, Looks like I'm going to be around for a while, Sam. Do you suppose you can get me better?"

"And that's the story of me getting almost killed in the hospital before you came," Kim said.

"Do you know you haven't stopped talking in fifty miles, Kim," Casey informed him.   "Well, I'm usually not this talkative but it is quite a story, you'll have to admit," Kim replied.   With that, Kim decided to take a nap.

C H A P T E R   5
AN INHERITANCE

⎵

From Denver they drove straight north to Wyoming, then turned west toward Laramie. By the time they reached Laramie, Kim woke up, needed to go to the bathroom and wanted something to eat.

Casey found a gas station and pulled in to fill up. It was a long way between gas stations in Wyoming and Casey knew enough to top off the tank whenever possible. If they hit a bad snowstorm and got stuck, for sure they wouldn't be able to walk out of it.

Every time they stopped, they had to get help extracting Kim from the truck cab and reinserting him. Going to the bathroom was no small problem with his hip-high cast. He had to have help sitting down and getting up. It was good he could wipe on his own because there was only so much Casey was willing to do.

The wind was blowing hard from the north and the road was slick. It was all Casey could do to hold the truck and trailer in his lane of the road. He started to stop so he could get out to relieve himself, but the wind started to blow the truck and trailer into the opposite lane. He decided he could hold it until they got to Rock Springs.

By the time they arrived in Rock Springs, Casey was totally exhausted. He was sleepy and weak after that long stay in the hospital. He decided they would stay overnight and make the hardest part of the drive the next day. The road from Rock Springs to Pinedale could be really bad if the north wind was blowing the loose snow. He wanted to be alert for that stretch.

Casey found a motel and registered. He knew he couldn't get Kim out of the truck alone so he asked the gal at the desk if she would help him. She was very accommodating. Between the two of them, they got Kim out and helped him to the room.

As they got to the door, Kim said, "You sure smell nice, honey. I could use a little nursing to get ready for bed and then I could use a little help in bed. Could you see your way clear to be a good ol' girl?"

"Kim, that's enough. This young lady was nice enough to help us. Don't repay her by insulting her."

"Insult! That was a compliment, not an insult," Kim returned.

"It may have been from your side, but I think it was an insult to her dignity."

"Thank you ma'am and good night," Casey said as he helped Kim to his bed.

She gave Kim a glance of interest and intrigue. Maybe he was wrong and Kim was the best judge of women, Casey thought.

"Hey partner, you can be your conscience, but don't be mine," Kim said. "I heard Rock Springs and Kemmerer used to be the relief for a cowboy's pent up desires. They say cowboys come from miles around to the red light district here."

"That's true Kim, but that ended thirty-five or forty years ago, long before this girl was born," Casey replied.

"That may be true, but I'll bet she wasn't offended like you think. She is probably wishing you hadn't got in the way," Kim said.

Casey didn't say anything, but he did wonder which one of them was right.

"Hell, Casey, I remember one time my best friend couldn't get away for a trip with his wife and another couple. He asked me to go in his place so his wife would have someone to go with."

"Now do you think I slept in an extra bed? Not on your life. We had a really good trip and I'm sure she didn't miss her husband."

"She praised me to him so much that he bought me and my gal a big meal when we went out with them. What he didn't know didn't hurt him and his wife was sure satisfied."

"Another time my pardner and I were driving across Wyoming. A snow storm was blowing so we decided to stop at the next ranch we came to before we got stuck."

"The next place we came to was a small ranch. It was quite a nice place but hadn't been kept up recently."

"As we drove up to the house, a nice looking, middle-aged lady came out the door."

"You never dismount when on horseback until you're asked so we just sat in the car waiting for an invitation to get out."

"'Is your husband around?' my pardner asked. She told us she had lost her husband in an accident last winter."

"What's the chance of putting us up, out of the snow storm for tonight?" I asked.

'"I wouldn't feel comfortable with you in the house, but you can stay in the bunk house if you would like,' she told us."

"We ate some snacks we had in the car, then went to sleep in our bed rolls. The next morning, we got up early and started our long drive to our next rodeo."

"My pardner came to see me a year and a half later. He had some questions for me."

"'Do you remember the time we stayed at that lady's ranch in Wyoming during that snow storm?' he asked me. 'I was contacted by that lady's lawyer.'"

"'What did her lawyer want anyway?' I asked him."

"My pardner said, 'Did you get up in the middle of the night and go bed down with her? Did you happen to use my name?'"

"Well, yes. I did go in and I did use your name, but she was real pleased when I left, I informed him."

"'That's why you wanted to get up and leave early that next morning, right?' he questioned."

"'Yeah, I didn't want her using your name or you both would have known,' I said."

"'Why, what could she be unhappy about?', I asked."

"'Oh, she wasn't unhappy. In fact, she was so pleased

that she left me everything she had when she died of the flu last month,' he told me."

"'Why, that is my inheritance, not yours. I was the one that pleased her, not you!' I told him."

"'Next time, use your own name if you want to get paid for your services,' he told me."

"Now what do you think of these women, Casey?"

Casey listened to all this but didn't have a thing to say. What did this guy use for a conscience? he thought.

CHAPTER 6

A HAY RIDE

U

The weather was better the next day. The wind had slowed down, at least for the morning.

Casey asked the morning desk clerk to help him get Kim into the truck. Luckily, it was a fellow, or who knows how long it would have taken to get Kim in.

The road had been plowed and the truck was handling quite well. All was going well so Casey started telling Kim some of the Old West history of the area. The hundred mile cattle trail drives from Pinedale to Rock Springs each fall were always good for some gab.

Casey said, "My great-grandfather helped open the Pinedale area for ranching."

Casey was proud of his heritage and loved living in this big ranching area, snuggled up next to the Wind River Range of mountains. This was a different range. This range ran southeast to northwest while other ranges ran north and south.

Casey knew of a peak nine thousand nine hundred and fifty feet high. It was named Tri-Basin Peak and was not well known by many. At this place, three drops of water falling an inch apart, will flow in three different directions: one drop will flow to the Great Salt Lake; another will go to the Snake River, then to the Columbia River and on to the Pacific Ocean;

the last drop will go to the Colorado River and end up in the Gulf of California, he told Kim.

Three drops of water have been recycling up and down for as long as the earth has been revolving around the sun. Our time on earth is so short compared to any other life form on earth. It's too bad that we waste so much of our time being sad.

Casey had tried to look on the bright side of his life. He knew he had it so much better than many others he knew. Yet he was still lonesome and looking for someone to fulfill his life. He wondered if he would ever find that special someone.

South of the ranch country was a semidesert with creeks and mesas. In the early spring cattle were grazed on the desert, then in early summer the cattle would move north into the lower hills. In the summer and fall they would graze the high mountains. This made for great ranching country in spite of the mosquitoes and horse flies through the summer.

"As you can see, the winters can be hard, but we don't have the wind with the cold. The towns south of us have strong winds all winter long."

"This is a good place to raise a family. There are so many good people who live here."

Kim soon started telling tales of his trails again. Most of his stories had a girl in them and an immoral moral.

Casey thought of all his adventures and misadventures but could not come up with anything that would fit into the conversation.

It wasn't long until they pulled into the ranch entrance. A mile down the lane, around a knoll, and up the draw sat the ranch house and out buildings.

Kim could see right off that this was a working cattle ranch and a big one at that. He was used to the small outfits back in Utah. His dad worked on a place with a hundred head of Hereford-Angus, crossed cattle. He had to work off the ranch half the time to keep food on the table. Kim had worked away from home most of the time to make extra money, but he still had to help his dad with their small acreage on the side.

"How big is this spread?" Kim asked.

"Oh, about five thousand deeded acres, plus the public range rights for a thousand head of mother cows."

"How many hired hands do you have?"

"In the winter we only have about five hands feeding cattle, then in spring we hire on more for calving. Haying requires another hiring," Casey said.

He continued, "A few of the winter feeders stay on as cowboys while others are used for equipment repair and haying."

They stopped up close to the front porch. Casey went in and came back out with a heavy built lady in her forties. She was the foreman's wife. She helped get Kim out of the truck and into the house. Casey thought he'd like to see Kim hit on her for a favor. She would knock him to the floor, cast and all.

That evening Kim met the family, the foreman and his

wife, and the hired hands. He was quite impressed with the size and scope of the outfit. He and Casey bedded down in the bunkhouse with the hired hands.

They laid around for a couple of days but were getting bored doing that. There was no way they could be of any help feeding or breaking horses, but they could possibly repair saddles and tack. Kim agreed in order to pay for his keep.

There were more than twenty saddles on racks in the barn tack room. There must have been forty bridles hanging on hooks around the walls. Casey taught Kim to make reins, repair saddles and sew leather. This was a good job for both of them because they were staying warm while the rest of the hands were out in the snow and cold feeding cattle.

February was over and March was just starting before Casey and Kim decided to go out on the sleigh to feed. Kim wanted to see the cattle and how feeding was handled in Wyoming. It was a warm day, with only a little wind, so they could stand being out.

Casey told Derk, the feeder, to let Kim drive the team. That was fine with Kim. He had driven a team a couple of times and figured he could easily handle that.

They went out over the bridge across the frozen creek. The trail was hard packed from the hay sleigh and horses packing it down each day. If the horses got off the trail they would sink to their bellies in the soft snow and get high centered.

Kim pulled the team up at the first gate and Derk jumped off to open it. Once the gate was opened, Kim spoke to the horses and they started through. Out of the willows trotted a big, bull moose with his head high and blowing through his nose. The team saw the moose and jumped sideways as they flew through the gate.

Sure enough, the horses were belly deep in snow; but worse than that, they took the gate post out and the next post broke off also. In the winter, there was no way to fix fences in four feet of snow on the level.

The horses were just standing still by then. They realized there was no place to go until they were dug out.

Derk took his shovel off the hayrack and started digging the team out. Casey was sure he was wondering why the two cripples hadn't stayed in the barn like they had done the past month.

"I've seen moose eating hay with the horses in the pasture next to the barn all winter," Kim said. "Why did these two fools spook when they saw this ol' feller?"

"It's just the way horses are. They can run with wild animals all the time and still spook when harnessed or saddled," Casey informed him.

Once the horses were dug out, Derk took the reins and spoke to the horses. They hit the tugs, but didn't move the sleigh which had slid part way off the trail. Taking down a stick with a leather whip on it, Derk popped the right horse and pulled the left line to bring them back on the trail. This time they hit it hard and up came the team with the sleigh following.

The jerk popped Kim. His hands didn't hold to the rack. He started falling and couldn't do anything to catch himself with the cast taking his balance away. The next thing he knew, he was floundering in four feet of fluffy, white snow. He felt like a big turtle on his back with no chance to right himself. Just like with the horses, Derk dug a path to Kim and around him. Derk helped Kim up and, with Casey's help from the wagon, they got him back on the sleigh.

"Looks like I'm more trouble than help out here. I guess I should have stayed at the barn," Kim said.

"Oh, don't worry about it," Casey said. "I have taken a gate post out myself. I remember the look I got from dad for it, too. You know, I'll bet he took a few out in his day."

They drove to the hay yard and up to the side of the haystack. With a hay saw, Derk sawed down through the frozen top hay and snow, then down through a section of the stack. He then started pitching hay onto the rack from the stack.

Kim had two good arms. Leaning against the front rack, he helped pack the hay on the sleigh. Casey couldn't use a fork with the cast on his arm that encased his elbow. He could walk around on the sleigh and pack the hay down.

Soon they had a load. Kim had stayed on the sleigh and stepped up as the load got higher. Casey climbed up the front bars of the sleigh so he could get up to Kim. Casey let Kim drive the team out of the stack yard. Derk shut the gates on each end of the stack yard after they pulled out. They drove to the feed grounds and started pitching hay off of each side as the team walked around the packed feed ground.

"I think I like feeding baled hay better than this loose hay," Kim said. "In Utah, most everyone bales their hay."

"We have been feeding cattle this way since the first hay was cut off these meadows. Some ranchers are trying bales, but we haven't changed. Dad is of the old school. He doesn't want to spend the money for those big tractors and balers. We do all our haying with teams and put it up loose," Casey said. "Some ranchers are trying the bales, but they have trouble cutting hay with tractors because of the mouse nests in the grass."

"You could cut your haying crew to one-fourth of what you use if you mechanized," Kim said.

"Yes, but Dad thinks these guys need a job and he likes having them around to tell stories about the 'good ol' days,'" Casey informed him. "I don't know if I would change if it was up to me. I enjoy the horses and hands."

The temperature had been thirty to forty below zero in February, but today it was up to ten degrees. This sunny day in March was considered a heat wave. That was one reason Casey and Kim decided to take a hay ride today. Soon, the cold would break and spring would start to appear.

CHAPTER 7

BAR HOPPING

U

It was the last of March and Kim was about to crawl the walls. He hadn't been out cattin' around for almost four months. That was a record for him.

"Hey Casey, let's go to town tonight. It's Saturday and the boys tell me there is always a good dance in the Stockman Bar."

"Well, I guess we could go in, but neither of us are in any shape to dance," Casey said.

"I just need to see a good-looking gal, even if I can't dance. Maybe we will get lucky and catch a couple," Kim said. "You know all the gals up here, don't you?"

"I know most of them, but most of those I know are married," Casey told him.

"So?" Kim said.

"So! We could get the rest of our bodies broke if we as much as look interested at someone's wife up here," Casey said.

"They're not that protective, are they?" Kim asked.

"Protective! They will fight if you happen to pick up the wrong beer let alone the wrong woman," Casey said. "It's even worse if they're not married so if we go in, you just keep control of yourself or someone else will."

They got all cleaned up for town and headed for the bar.

"There are three bars in town. Why don't we go bar hopping?" Kim questioned.

"That bar on the far east block is one of those where you stagger in and get drug out. The Cowboy Bar across the street is a walk in, stagger out bar. The Stockman Bar is a walk in walk out bar," Casey said.

"Oh, you mean this is a higher class establishment. Is that what you're saying, Casey?"

"You might say that," Casey replied.

People were already dancing. It looked like everyone was friendly and having fun. Kim and Casey sat down at an empty table and ordered a drink. Of course, Kim had to make a pass at the bar girl.

"Now remember what I told you, Kim. I can't help you if you get in trouble," Casey reminded him.

It wasn't long until two guys and their gals came over. Kim could see the girls were both trim-cut critters. His blood was starting to rise.

"We heard you were back, Casey. Sure glad you made out okay at the hospital," the tall fellow said.

"I'll be fine as soon as I get this damn cast off, Brad," Casey replied.

"Oh, by the way," Casey said, "this is Kim Randall from Utah. I met him in the hospital and we're recuperating at the ranch together."

"Howdy, Kim," Brad said. "This is Johnny, Sue and Candy. Johnny is from Oklahoma. I think he has had all the winter he wants. He's ready to go back down south. Candy and Sue are working in the Cowboy Shop, selling duds."

"Where are you girls from?" Kim asked.

"Oh, I'm from Idaho Falls and she's from Jackson," Candy said. "We came over here to get away from home and have fun."

"I'll bet this is the place to do it, too," Kim said.

"Sit down and join us," Casey said.

They all pulled up a chair and sat down. Candy sat next to Kim and with six around a small table, they were in close proximity to each other.

The talk was all about Casey and his fight in Denver. Kim was getting tired of Casey getting all the attention.

"Well, I tangled with a two-ton piece of steel and a hundred-pound girl to get my badge of plaster," Kim said.

"How far up does that cast go on your leg, Kim?" Candy asked.

"Not far enough to stop me from enjoying life," Kim said.

Candy looked a little pink at the answer. Casey quickly changed the subject to Johnny and Oklahoma.

Kim's knee was now pressed against Candy's leg. To his surprise, she didn't move it but rather pushed toward him.

Candy looked Kim right in the eye and Kim got the message. She was charged about as much as he was . . . if that was possible.

Johnny also noticed the look. He shrugged it off as unimportant. Soon he realized that there were more looks between them.

"Excuse me, Mister, but that is my date you are making eyes at," Johnny said. "In my country that is not good etiquette."

"Well, it's good we're not in your country then, isn't it?" Kim replied.

"Don't take offense Johnny," Casey said. "He's been in a hospital or at the ranch for too long. He is really harmless."

However, Casey knew that wasn't a good excuse for Kim's actions. He knew Kim wasn't really harmless for any girl at any time.

"Candy, let's dance," Johnny said.

"No, I don't want to dance right now. You go get someone else to dance with," Candy replied.

"Okay, if that's the way you want it," Johnny said as he stood up and turned to leave.

"I'll watch out for Candy for you if you want," Kim said as Johnny walked away without an answer.

Brad, Sue and Casey were discussing calving problems and the possibility of a warm spell to help the young ones make it through.

Kim and Candy were getting acquainted, too. Kim had two good hands and he had them all over Candy. She really couldn't have cared less about stopping him.

Kim looked up to see Johnny standing over him, "If you didn't have that cast on, I would wipe the floor with you."

"Then it's a good thing I do have it for both of us, isn't it?" Kim said.

"I think we'd better leave now," Casey said.

"Okay, Casey, but can I take Candy with me? I'm sure she's tired of this place."

"It seems like we've been through this before. No! You're going back to the ranch with me," Casey said.

"Okay, you're the boss, but I'd rather just go across the street," Kim said.

Casey helped Kim up and they turned to leave. "We'll be in the bar across the street, Candy, if you get lonely," Kim announced over his shoulder as they were leaving.

It wasn't fifteen minutes before Candy walked in and said, "Mind if I sit down?"

"No, sit right here," Kim said as he slid a chair close to his.

Without Johnny around, the necking got hot and heavy for being right out in front of everyone, but then who in this bar would give a damn?

Casey got up and walked over to the pool table. He really wasn't watching the game but was rather deep in thought.

What is it that attracts the girls to this guy? From what he'd seen, he wasn't so sure all those stories were just tales. It looked like they may have been true.

When he looked around, Kim and Candy were no where in sight. Their drinks were only half finished and he was sure that would be the only thing that was left half finished.

Casey talked with some of the local ranchers and hired hands while he waited for Kim to return. Suddenly a hand was on his shoulder turning him around.

"Johnny! What do you want?"

"Candy," Johnny replied. "Where is she?"

"To be right down honest with you, I don't know, Johnny. Sit down and have a drink," Casey said.

Johnny was about two thirds tight now and didn't want to sit down. He wanted a fight and that was real plain to see.

"That friend of yours is going to get his other leg broke, when I find him. You can bank on that. Nobody takes my girl away from me, especially not a gimp like him," Johnny said and walked out the door.

The first time in town and Kim was in trouble. Casey could see the problem wasn't going to go away. He had to do something about it.

About an hour had passed when Kim and Candy came back to the bar.

"Candy, Johnny's looking for you," Casey said.

"Johnny who?" Candy said. "I'm with Kim tonight."

"I don't think that's a good idea, Candy. Johnny has blood in his eyes and he aims to have a piece of Kim's hide," Casey said.

"He can't have a piece 'cause I want them all," Candy said with a girly giggle.

"You know, Candy, my last gal wanted me to change in three ways. Women are like that. They always want to change something about a man, even the best man. She didn't like the way I kept an eye on my boots as I walked. Well, my old dad told me to 'watch my step.' She didn't like me picking my nose. Dad told me to 'keep my nose clean,' and I always follow my dad's heeding. The biggest thing she bitched about was I wouldn't let her get on top when we made love. That was one thing dad was adamant about. He said, 'whatever you do, don't screw up.'"

Then, turning to Casey, Kim said, "You know, Casey, I just didn't heed his schooling on one of those tonight."

Just then, Johnny stepped back through the door. "Mister, you have a whipping coming so stand up," Johnny said.

"Now it looks like I screwed up for the second time tonight," Kim said.

Candy ran toward Johnny but was caught with a back hand that sent her to the floor. Blood was coming out of her nose and the corner of her lip.

"Now, you shouldn't have done that cowboy," Casey said as he stood up.

Johnny took three long steps across the floor before he reached Casey. A looping right swing went past Casey's head as he ducked down. Using his good left hand, Casey hit Johnny in the stomach, bending him over in pain and sickness. Down came his right with the cast to the back of Johnny's head and that ended that.

"Get up and get out to the truck," Casey ordered Kim.

"Some of you boys look after Johnny, will you?" Casey said. "I didn't hit him hard so he'll be okay in a minute."

Helping Candy up, he said, "You better get home before you get hurt worse than you already are. You played a dirty game and maybe you got your dues. I don't like to see a man hit a woman no matter how wrong she is, but next time there might not be any help."

Kim was getting strong enough to help himself into the truck by now so Casey went around and got in. Kim slid in and shut the door.

"Well, you sure took care of that Okie, didn't you?" Kim said.

"It sure wasn't for you," Casey answered.

"I could have cleaned his plow with or without this cast," Kim said.

"Maybe and maybe not, but that isn't the real problem. You can't control yourself and I'm not going to be involved in your escapades," Casey said.

"I'll be good, boss. Just give me another chance," Kim chided.

"Okay, but if this happens again, you're going down the road, friends or not," Casey assured Kim.

"We'll have these casts off soon and we can hit the rodeo trail again partner," Kim said.

"I'm not sure I'm going back this year," Casey said, almost surprising himself. He had been roping and cutting on the circuit for the past five years and had done tolerably well. Maybe it was time to stay home and take over some of the responsibility of running the ranch.

C H A P T E R 8
CASTS OFF

U

Spring was moving in. The cows were about ready to calve and the snow was melting around the drifts. The willows were turning reddish purple with new growth starting to bud out.

It was time for the casts to come off Kim and Casey. They were both anxious to get them off. Kim had a clothes hanger straightened out and his hide was red from scratching. Casey had kept nipping away at his arm cast until he had better movement of his wrist and shoulder. They had been exercising the rest of their bodies, trying to build up their strength and endurance.

Casey's heart rate rose quickly at first as he tried to exercise, but he kept it up day after day until his recovery time decreased. Kim was a little lazy about his exercises, but he was young and quite fit.

They were going to have to drive down to Rock Springs to be checked with an x-ray and then have the casts cut off. Casey arranged to take a ranch pickup with an automatic shift so it would be easier to drive.

The drive was a lot easier this time than it was in January. Water was running down the sides of the road and the smell of sage was in the air. The sky was mostly sunny with a few billowing, white clouds. It was warm in the truck and that felt good.

Kim could generally sleep easily when he got in the truck. This day was no different. About five miles south of Pinedale, Kim was sound asleep. Casey found himself alone for all practical purposes.

Driving from one rodeo to another had given Casey a lot of time to think about life and what he wanted out of it. Looking over at the sleeping Kim, Casey knew they had very different expectations out of life.

Casey had seen Kim's loose morals and the little respect he showed for others' feelings. He hadn't seen Kim shed tears. He either was able to control his emotions at will or had shallow feelings.

It was hard for Casey to hide his feelings. He wished he could be in control of his emotions to a greater extent but just wasn't able to. Casey tried not to get too close to the gals he dated. He was looking for the right woman; he felt he would know when the chemistry and inward desires were right.

Kim was sleeping like a baby. He had no problems troubling him. He was content with the world and didn't care who knew it.

Rock Springs was busy. Kim woke up quickly as Casey stopped at the bottom of the off ramp.

"You slept for almost two hours," Casey informed Kim. "Have you ever ridden in a car when you didn't sleep?"

"Only when there was an attractive driver I could hit on and you sure don't fit the bill," Kim replied.

"How about keeping your hands to yourself while we are

here," Casey requested. "Why? Does it bother you?" Kim asked.

"Yes, it does bother me and I don't want to get in another fight over it. If you need it so much, there is still a red light district here," Casey informed him.

"You think I'm going to pay for a woman. I don't have to pay for what I want when women want it, too," Kim shot back.

"Well, just stay out of trouble," Casey ordered.

At 3:00 P.M., they were at the doctor's office. "Which one of you wants to be first?" a nurse asked.

"I'll go first," Kim said. "I can't wait to scratch where I couldn't reach."

"That's fine with me," Casey said.

In an hour, they both had their casts sawed off. Kim had his new jeans on for the first time in months. Casey was able to get a shirt over both arms and button it up. They both looked like normal guys.

"Let's go get some dinner," Kim suggested.

"That sounds like a good idea," Casey said. They stopped at a nice looking restaurant which advertised steak specials.

"I feel like I can eat a whole cow," Kim said.

"I'm hungry, too. I hope they can cook a steak well done," Casey replied.

They entered the restaurant and saw a sign which said, "The waitress will seat you."

"This must be a high class place if you have to have help

getting seated. I could have used it when I had my cast; now I think I can seat myself," Kim said.

The waitress came over and said, "Follow me."

They sat down at a table near the far end of the room. Kim took the chair closest to the wall. Casey sat across from him.

"If you want dinner you will have to wait until 5:00 P.M.," the waitress informed them.

"That's thirty minutes," Kim stated. "What time do you serve supper if dinner starts at 5:00 P.M.?" Kim asked.

"We'll have a drink and wait until five to have our dinner," Casey told her. "Give us each a Pepsi."

"I'd still like to know when they serve supper if dinner starts at five," Kim jokingly chided.

"On the ranch, there is a breakfast, dinner at noon, and supper after work," Casey told the waitress.

"When do you have lunch?" she asked.

"We have a full meal at each seating at the table. Lunch is not a part of our agenda," Casey told her.

"That could make for fat cowboys," she said.

"Not when you work as hard as cowboys do," he informed her.

They each had a big steak and enjoyed the well-cooked meat, especially when they looked around and saw the blood on the plates around them.

That night they took a walk around town. There was a full moon so they could see fairly well. As they reached a two-story brick building, they heard a lot of noise. Just as they passed the last door, a body came through it.

"What's going on in there?" Kim asked.

"That's the Elk's Lodge and they're holding an Elk's ball," Casey informed him.

"Boy, if they don't let go, they'll all be killed," Kim chided.

Casey thought that might be more truth than fiction, the way it was sounding.

It was in the second bar that Kim found a gal about as horny as he was. Again, she was with someone else. It didn't take long until Kim had her attention. He had her boyfriend's attention, too.

"Kim, anything you get into, you will have to get out of, by yourself," Casey told him.

It seemed strange for the smaller statured cowboy to be telling this almost six-foot cowboy how to take care of himself.

"Don't worry, partner, I'll take care of myself," Kim told him.

Sure enough, here it came.

"Are you flirting with my girl?" this big, outdoor-looking, middle-aged guy said.

"I thought she was flirting with me," Kim replied.

"I wasn't."

"Oh, shut up. I saw you, too," he said.

Pointing to Casey, Kim said, "This is my body guard, so

don't get too mouthy."

Casey got up and started to walk away. The big guy reached out for Casey's arm when all hell broke loose. Kim popped him on his upper arm muscle which momentarily paralyzed his arm. With three more well placed punches, the big man went down.

Kim grabbed the girl's arm and out the door the three went.

"I'm going to the motel, Kim. You better get one of your own tonight. I'm leaving early so you better be here," Casey informed him.

Off Kim ran with the girl in tow.

The next morning, Kim was waiting at the restaurant for Casey. There were few words spoken. The ride home was no more vocal because Kim slept most of the way. He looked to Casey like a man that hadn't got too much rest the night before.

CHAPTER 9

TWO STYLES

Now that their casts were off, Kim and Casey could start putting time in on the colts. Being a rough stock rider, Kim hadn't developed the finesse with horses that Casey had since he trained cutting and roping horses while Kim was riding broncs.

Their first job on horseback was to ride through the cow herds. They would bring in the cows that were ready to calve and those that had just calved. The pregnant cows would be kept in a pasture with sheds so they would have a windbreak. All the cows with new calves were put in a different pasture so they could be fed additional hay.

Casey rode with Kim for a few days and showed him how to pull a calf when needed. The young heifers had a harder time calving than the older cows so the men had to watch them closer and make sure they would have help if they needed it.

Pulling calves took a lot of compassion and softness so that the heifers would accept the intrusion into this very disruptive time of their lives. Casey had helped with calving since he was a boy. His Dad had shown him how to rub the heifers and relax them before he went to work. Aggression only created fear and mistrust. Casey had the right personality for the job. He enjoyed helping a heifer give birth, watching as the calf was licked dry before it got up and nursed its mother.

He always felt like he had a hand in God's plan.

Kim didn't take too well to the midwife stuff. The heifers wouldn't stay quiet while he tried to help them. He usually ended up bringing them to the corral where he could get help.

This was not a job Kim enjoyed so he was glad when the cows were calved out. He knew there were a lot of other jobs he would rather have.

Casey cut out three horses for each of them one Monday morning.

"It looks like we've got our work cut out for us. These colts are three years old. They have been handled some but they haven't really enjoyed man up 'til now," Casey told Kim.

"Why do you wait so long to break them?" Kim asked.

"In this country, horses grow a lot slower than in warmer climates. It takes all of their feed in the winter for maintenance and warmth so there's no feed left for growth until it warms up. It takes them four years to be developed enough to break," Casey told him.

Casey remembered back to when the horses purchased and raised were descendants of the wild herds down in the south desert. Now they raised their colts from well-bred mares and top stallions. This gave the colts a gentleness which was bred into them. The colts were fed up better than the range-type horses used to be. They were never mistreated. They were branded with a freeze brand which left a nice white brand which was easy to see and caused no pain to the horse.

The colts were tranquilized when they were gelded. This reduced the stress from this procedure. In the earlier days, the colts were tied down and they strained so hard that all their muscles would get sore. They wouldn't want to exercise so they would swell more. They had a much harder time getting over the gelding process.

Casey exercised the colts in the round corral now so the colts had little swelling. This gentled them down early in life so they were much easier to break.

Casey remembered how they used to rope a four or five year old gelding and choke him until he passed out. At that moment, a halter with a long rope was put on him. A rope was tied around the colt's neck and a hind foot was tied up to it so the colt couldn't step down on that leg. This took his mobility away. The colt would gasp for air and gain his footing but would find he couldn't run away. Then the bronc buster could sack the colt out with a blanket. After that, the colt was curried down, his tail was pulled, and the snarls were pulled out of his mane.

This was a lot for a colt to handle on the first encounter with the bronc buster, but that wasn't all. They were saddled and rode that first encounter. The horse was scared so he bucked. Very few could go through this without trying to get the bronc buster off their back. Most bucked hard for a week or so. Soon they mellowed out and gentled down with a lot of wet saddle blankets, or a lot of hard, long rides. Some never quit bucking. They had to be topped out each time they were going to be used.

Many of the colts were being used before they were even

completely halter broke. This meant the cowboy would have to dismount at a gate, open it, mount up to ride through the gate, then dismount to close the gate.

Some colts liked to buck each time the rider mounted so the colt had to take a couple jumps, then the rider could ride him up to the gate, so he could get off and close it. This was the hard way to break horses, both for the horse and the rider.

Cowboys got a lot of practice riding bucking horses. The good riders faired well, but the cowboys who couldn't keep their balance soon decided to change their occupation while they were still alive.

"I don't know how you break horses, but I just get on and ride them," Kim said.

"Well, I like to take it a little slower. I want to form a bond of trust with my horse. I want him to think I am good for him and not his nemesis," Casey said.

"I'll break mine my way and you break yours your way, and we'll see how they come out," Kim suggested.

"No, I don't need any bucking horses. I need gentle ranch horses. These horses are well bred and don't need to be rough handled. They need a friend and a chance to learn," Casey informed him.

"Have it your way, but it sure is a lot quicker my way. If they know they will get punished if they don't do what I want, they are going to respond quicker when I tell them," Kim said.

"You may be right, but I want a horse to do what I ask

to please me, not out of fear. If I get in a possible wreck, I want him to listen to me and trust my judgement instead of being afraid and freaking out when I need him to be calm," Casey said.

It wasn't long before Casey noticed Kim just wasn't giving the colts a chance to cooperate. He was putting so much pressure on them so the only reaction they could see was to fight.

"Kim, why don't you take a day and just give these colts a good massage. Rub them on their heads, over their eyes and over their nose. Scratch them under the chin. Rub them over the neck, back and down their legs. Let them feel how you can make them comfortable. It really will make a difference," Casey told him.

Casey's colts were mellowing down, accepting being sacked out and working well on the longe line. Casey had them working off his words: Walk, Trot, Whoa, Come Here and Stand. He knew the horse learned quicker from voice commands than any other cue.

It was peculiar for Kim to watch Casey's colts come up to him in the corral and stick their noses on him and up to his face. Kim could see these colts liked Casey. His colts showed no such interest in him. He had to corner each one before he could catch them. He really didn't like them and found it hard to try to show them he did. He had always used horses as a tool to get cow work done, never as a friend or partner; and he didn't feel like changing now.

After three weeks, Casey had started riding his colts without having them buck. Kim's colts had all bucked when he started riding them. They were still jumpy and unsettled.

"Why don't you wear your spurs Casey? You could get them to turn and handle much quicker," Kim said.

"I see your colts wringing their tails. That is because they are afraid of your feet."

"I want them to be afraid of my spurs, so they will jump when I tell them to jump," Kim replied.

"The colt can't be afraid of you. He must trust your legs. They give him support and strength. They give him confidence and trust in you and in themselves," Casey said.

Kim didn't want to out-think the horse. He wanted to manhandle him and force him to work. He didn't need the colt's friendship; and he sure didn't want to spend anymore time playing like Casey did.

"Casey, I think I am going to go back home and start hitting some rodeos. I need to get practice and I'm not getting any around here. I'll ride the colts the rest of the week, then I'll be headin' down the road," Kim said.

"If that's what you want, then that's what you should do," Casey told him.

"Come Saturday morning, Kim was packed and ready to pull out. He was well again and wanted to get on with his life. Casey thought it was probably a good idea because Kim wasn't gaining anything at the ranch and neither were the colts.

"Well, Kim, I hope you had a good rest up here. You look healthy and ready to take on the world. Take care and don't get busted up again. Maybe I will see you on the circuit again sometime," Casey said.

"I do feel fit," Kim replied. "I just need more action than you have around here. I need the circuit to keep me pumped up. I guess I'm not a horse trainer or a cow tender. I like the adrenaline rush of sitting down on a big bull or outwitting some guy and taking his girl. That's what keeps me wired and ready to fire. I need that to keep me sharp. Look me up when you get down my way," he said as he got in his pickup and pulled out.

CHAPTER 10

PICKING HORSES AND WIVES

U

It was a pleasantly warm day for riding across open country to drive cattle to the upper ranch twenty-five miles above the main ranch. Casey hadn't really missed Kim, but he did feel he needed a companion. He had had partners, friends, and even a few girl friends; but he had only found one woman he thought he could enjoy living with forever.

Casey remembered how Kim treated women and how some really got turned on by him. They weren't the kind of women he wanted. So how was he to find a wife?

What would I do if I wanted a special horse, Casey thought. First, I would advertise for what I wanted. Maybe that's what he should do, he thought.

A cow tried to quit the herd so he rode out around her and pushed her back. It didn't take much thinking to do the job. The horse he was riding was an experienced cow horse and could about do the job by himself. It left Casey a lot of time to think.

That's it, I will put an ad in the newspaper when I get back to town. The next day was Friday so Casey went to town and put an ad in the paper which read:

Wanted, a woman interested in horses and horsemen. Needs to be fit and capable of riding horses and interested in cross-country and down-

hill skiing. Do you want to live the western life? No smoking or drinking and believe in God. If you fit this description, call me at (307) 814-0106.

To Casey's surprise, only two women called. He set up a dinner date for each of them. The first looked years beyond the years she admitted to. The other smelled of cigarette smoke and neither of them would he be willing to take to a dog fight, let alone a horse sale. He could see the women who read the personal ad in the local paper were not his kind. Maybe he could reach more women if he advertised in a horse magazine. He knew of one magazine which fit the bill.

Casey worked up an ad which looked like it might bring the response he hoped for.

Mature Horse Oriented Gals

I'm looking for a wife. I'm lonesome and it's hard to meet the type of gal I'm looking for. I'm 5'8", 150 pounds and fit. I train horses, ride in the hills and enjoy the Western life. I also cross country and downhill ski. I enjoy leather arts and am open to other activities. I'm looking for a fit, attractive gal that can ride and can or would be interested in learning to ski. One that would feel comfortable wearing boots and Western wear and sharing the Western life. No smoking or drinking. I have a ranch in Wyoming. If you fit the profile and are interested please call (307) 814-0106.

Once he questioned the women about their interests, age, color of eyes and weight, he could do like he did when he went to a horse sale. First he would take the catalog and mark off all those that were the wrong gender. He hoped he didn't need to do that. Then he would mark off those that were too old or too young. Lastly, would be to mark off the ones that were too short or too tall. He didn't want one that was too stocky either.

When Casey was looking for a horse, he always wanted eye appeal. He like horses that were wide between the eyes and kind looking. Most horses have brown eyes, but Casey wanted a blue-eyed woman. He felt he could look inside the soul of blue eyes but was shut out by dark eyes.

He remembered again what the ranch foreman once told him: "Select a wife like you do a horse. She should have eye appeal, a well-rounded hip, be V-ed up well in the chest with enough bone to handle the work." That stuck in his mind.

Now all he had to do was to search this gal out. He had received twenty-four calls and had asked all the important questions. Most answered the questions, but a few said these were questions you didn't ask a woman. Mostly that went for the age and weight questions. If he didn't get an answer, he presumed he wouldn't have wanted her anyway. One was quite young and got upset when Casey told her she was too young. One gal was one hundred eighty pounds and five foot three inches tall.

Then there was one with sixty mares to foal out. Another had four top bred stallions she stood. If she liked studs, maybe he wouldn't measure up. Another was raising and showing working cow horses and Casey didn't want to be tied into someone else's agenda.

As Casey listened to each voice and read through their answers, he realized only one woman interested him. He had gone to a lot of sales and only bought one horse. Sometimes he never found one he liked and felt good about going home empty.

When it came right down to it, there was only one woman that sounded like she would fit the bill. That wasn't a very good group to choose from, but he was really lonesome so he thought he would take a chance. He made a date for the next Saturday, but by Wednesday he was going crazy wondering what she was like so he called her and made a date for the next day. She had to make up a story to get the day off work. She worked at Wal-Mart and said they were quite strict when asked for an extra day off.

Casey met her at a saddle shop in Salt Lake City which was located between their two towns but much closer to her.

When they met, they were both driving pickup trucks. That was a good sign, Casey thought. They talked for over an hour and found they had a lot in common. She had horses and dogs, and she stated some of the same feelings he had about animals. They were both hungry so they went and had supper.

Casey made an appointment to meet her the next weekend at a horse sale. They looked over the catalog and the horses and found they agreed on the best horses in the sale.

Casey realized he didn't really remember what she looked

like. She had a nice shape, blonde hair and blue eyes. Her voice was sweet and she was easy to talk to. Her name was Vanna. He had had a mare named Vanna, but he couldn't really put a face on her.

On the next date, they went to a movie and watched "Sea Biscuit" win the races. They both shed tears. Casey could see they were both soft hearted. This was a short meeting, but they were getting to know each other.

Casey hadn't hugged or kissed her yet, but he knew he liked her personality. He could tell she was getting interested, too. She reminded him, in some ways, of the gal that got away some years back.

Casey knew he was very interested in her. During the next visit, she showed him her stallion. He was only fourteen hands and very thick necked, but he could see her stallion was really bonded to her. Casey hoped she would bond that closely to him. On this visit, he got a hug.

Casey attended most of the horse sales in the adjacent states. He arranged for Vanna to meet him at the sale in her area. He was real anxious to see her again. It was funny but he still didn't have a picture of her in his mind. Was she beautiful or common? He really didn't know. He just knew he was infatuated with her and couldn't wait to spend time with her. He was very lonesome and had enjoyed the time he had spent with her.

While they were at the sale, a horse breeder and trainer came up to Casey and told him he should check out Vanna's background. He told Casey that she had been married twice and lived with an older fellow for five years after that.

Casey thought about it but didn't worry enough about it. He asked Vanna about it and why she hadn't told him. She said she was going to tell him. She said she was a born again Christian and had changed her life around.

Casey was so enthralled with her, he didn't pay much heed to what this could mean or why she didn't stay married.

Their next date was to another horse sale five hours away. This was a big sale with a lot of good geldings. All the way out to the sale, they talked about everything and anything. It was a great trip. This gal was so sweet and so enjoyable to be with. He knew they were going to get along great.

They watched the sale preview and looked the horses over. They each picked three horses they were the most interested in. It just so happened, they were the same three out of one hundred and sixty head.

As the sale started, the prices were very high. Casey wondered how he would ever buy one of the three they picked. By the time their second choice came around, he was getting pretty worried. He had a policy of not buying a horse for more than the horse would bring if resold. He always tried to look beyond what the horse was at the sale. He evaluated the horse, using his economic principles to work. Casey figured there were four economic principles that could change the value of a horse: 1) Time of sale, like buying in the winter and selling in the spring, 2) Change the place of sale, like buying in an area with too many horses and selling where there weren't enough horses, 3) Change the appearance of the horse, like shedding him out or feeding him up, and 4)

Changing the function of the horse, like training him more or training for a specific function. He kinew that one, or all, of these economic principles could make a profit for a shrewd horseman.

The bidding started on lot #18, their second choice. Casey didn't bid until the bidding stopped. It was his principle not to push the bid up, but rather wait until the bidding stopped. Then he knew about what he was going to have to pay.

Casey bid twice and bought the horse at a price which was cheap for the second best horse in the sale.

When their third choice came in the ring the prices had gotten even higher. It seemed like the first horses were a little slower selling. No one was going to pay too much until they saw what the market looked like.

This horse was the horse Vanna wanted. She thought it was a lost cause because the bid was already over three thousand three hundred dollars, but the bidding had stopped so Casey bid once and bought him. His bid had been just a dip of his hat so she didn't know he was the buyer until they asked for his bid card number. She was elated when she discovered Casey had bought the horse. Now she had a horse to come and ride at the ranch. Casey figured that would be good enough for a kiss. It had been so long since he had kissed a gal. The only one he had ever really loved had other commitments so he couldn't have her even after they fell in love. It was a no- win situation, but he still held her memory very dear to him and compared every woman to her. She had been a horse lover too and Casey thought this gal was a lot like she was.

The 85th lot was their first pick. He was a dapple gray with a good body and a kind eye. He looked much like the lot 18 that he had bought. This horse hadn't had as much training as the other two, and it was later in the sale. The prices were getting even higher. The gray horse sold for four thousand five hundred dollars so Casey let him go. He already had two of the top horses in the sale.

After the sale, they fed the two horses and went into town for supper. They had only eaten a hot dog for dinner and were ready for something more.

Casey had shown Vanna how fast he made decisions to buy horses now he was going to show her how fast he would ask her to marry him. That night, as they laid on the bed watching TV, he popped the question. Vanna was shocked and couldn't figure out how he could make a decision so quickly. She wasn't sure he was serious.

Casey thought maybe she was gun shy after having three relationships before him. He didn't want to make a mistake either but felt she was right for him. They had adjoining bedrooms so they went to bed after a long talk. Vanna didn't give him an answer on that trip.

The next weekend, Casey drove down to Vanna's home in central Utah. He didn't know what to expect from her parents and siblings. He found her parents very reserved and not warm at all. In fact, they were cool. Her sister was luke warm and easy to talk to. Her two brothers were reserved and not that friendly. They all had been divorced once or twice.

Casey told her he was interested in marrying her but not

her family. That didn't set too well with her, but then she told him her parents weren't warm to her growing up. They never told her they loved her. She had had a hard time feeling and showing real love.

When Casey finally met Vanna's two married sons, he found they both had been divorced too. They were very cool and didn't speak more than ten words to him on their first meetings despite talking to each other profusely with him in the room. It was like he wasn't even there.

This wasn't the way Casey was used to relating to people. He was outgoing and enjoyed his friends and acquaintances.

Vanna agreed to marry Casey on their next meeting. Casey was real happy about this union, but there was something in the back of his mind that told him to take some precautions. Before the marriage, he prepared a prenuptial agreement which would give Vanna twenty thousand dollars a year for each year they were married if he asked for a divorce and half that if she asked for a divorce. If he died, she would get half a million dollars in insurance.

HUSBAND BEATER

U

_____

Casey and Vanna were married and moved to an attractive small ranch close to his parent's ranch. He had saved much of what he made working, trading horses and competing. He never learned how to enjoy spending money, just how to make it. He had bought and sold horses over the years and it had been financially good for him. He had a big bank account and his parents had given him some land for his marriage. He let Vanna sign for the home, but not any land.

On the other hand, Vanna had worked and lived with her parents of late. She spent more than she made. She had a credit card that was maxed out. She had recently bought a fairly new Dodge pickup and paid plenty for it.

Casey gave Vanna three thousand dollars to pay off her credit card. He made her promise never to charge more than she could pay the next month so there was no interest to pay.

She had a three hundred-dollar monthly payment on her truck so Casey told her he would give her five hundred dollars a month. Three hundred dollars was to pay on her truck and two hundred to spend. He also got her some health insurance which wasn't cheap.

Casey didn't like the idea of paying high interest on the truck. They didn't need the truck because Casey had a newer pickup and a nice car so they decided to sell Vanna's pickup.

Casey paid the nineteen thousand dollars owing on the truck, then put it up for sale. It just wouldn't sell so he dropped the price to sixteen thousand dollars and sold it. He lost another three thousand dollars.

Now Vanna would not need the three hundred dollars for the truck payment. He suggested he drop her monthly allotment. She would have none of that so he gave her five hundred a month to just spend to keep peace in the family. This was a strain on their short marriage. Casey wasn't used to seeing money squandered.

Casey had worked hard for his money and had spent little. He couldn't understand her purchases of knick-knacks and decorations for all the holidays. She spent all five hundred dollars each month and used her credit card too. She never let him see her credit card bill. That upset him, too.

Casey and Vanna rode horses a lot at first. Vanna had told Casey about her competition in the horse arena and on the track. She had won Western Pleasure trophies and rode race horses out of the gates. Yet when Roany, the horse from the sale, would shy a little she would get upset. She wanted to sell Roany and get a gray or buckskin that would be more quiet. She never tried to bond with Roany so he didn't care much for her.

When it came to leads, she didn't know one from the other and she didn't want Casey telling her how to ride. She liked moving cattle so they spent many hours working cows. Casey tried to make her happy, or at least content.

Vanna spent a lot of time in the yard planting flowers. She had all kinds of pretty flowers that made the yard look great. She kept the house up and did the wash, but she wouldn't iron one thing for Casey so he kept on ironing his own clothes.

She soon began requesting that Casey put her name on his checking account and other bank holdings. She had her own checking account and a sixty-five hundred dollar money market account. Casey was used to having his separate account for his horse business and didn't want her writing checks on it.

Casey finally put Vanna's name on his checking account and on a one hundred thousand dollar money market account. A week later, his banker pulled him to the side and asked him if he really wanted to put his wife's name on that much money until he was married a little longer. He told Casey to remember, she could withdraw the whole one hundred thousand dollars without his permission.

After thinking about how aggressive she was about getting her name on the money, he decided to take Vanna off the money market account and make it so she could only withdraw from the checking account if he died. He even took her name off the car, pickup, horse trailer and four wheelers. That didn't set well with Vanna. She went to Casey's mother and asked if she thought he should put her name on the accounts because they should be partners in everything. Casey's mother told her that none of her friends that remarried shared everything.

Casey wanted to please Vanna so he bought a beautiful palomino gelding. She wouldn't ride him so Casey now had another horse that needed work. He put more training on the palomino. Finally Vanna decided she would ride him. As they rode across the pasture, something happened. The palomino kicked up his back feet and twisted a little. Off came Vanna. She wasn't hurt, but they turned around and headed for the barn. That was the last time she rode the palomino.

With a little work, Casey sold the palomino and made fifteen hundred dollars more than he gave for him. Vanna was sure she should have half of what they made on horses. Casey told her she hadn't added any value to the horse so he couldn't see where she had anything extra coming. The money went into the horse account for future purchases. Maybe he was wrong to feel this way, but Vanna just wasn't any help with the horses.

Next, he bought a beautiful dapple gray for her. She once again refused to ride this horse so Casey put some training on him and found a buyer who paid considerably more. Again Vanna wanted her share. The dream of a soul mate faded fast as their horse riding wasn't even enjoyable and the western life was just a decoration of the house, not an inner feeling.

It was a good thing Casey made money trading horses and working on the ranch because Vanna didn't use a penny of the sixty five hundred dollar money market she had stashed away for the betterment of their relationship.

That fall, after the haying was done, Casey's mother's sister asked Casey if he and Vanna would like a paid vacation to go to Arizona and clean out their winter trailer home which they had sold. Casey's uncle had been sick for the past two years so they weren't able to travel south anymore.

This sounded like a good deal so they hooked up the horse trailer and got ready to go. Their instructions were to clean out the personal belonging and a few pieces of furniture and leave the rest. One item they were most concerned about was a 1959 Barbie doll still in the box on the bedroom shelf. It was now worth over ten thousand dollars. They had to leave so fast the year before she forgot to get it.

Casey and Vanna had a nice trip going down to Arizona. They spent time in Wickenburg where some of Casey's friends lived in the winter. This was a western town with a lot of retired horse people. Casey had hopes of getting out of the cold in the winter but knew that was a long way off with a ranch to help run.

When they arrived at Quartzite, Arizona, Casey went right to the storage room and started packing things. Vanna went into the bedroom and started packing there.

It took them all that evening and the next morning to get everything packed and loaded in the trailer. As they were about ready to pull away, Casey asked Vanna if she had found the Barbie doll. Vanna informed him she hadn't seen it when she packed that bedroom. Casey was very concerned so he called his aunt. She told him there was only one other person who had a key and she trusted her implicitly.

Casey was very concerned that she might think he had taken it. That was a lot of money and would tempt many people, but Casey was not tempted in the least.

On the way home, Vanna wanted Casey to drive thirty miles out of their way to see her son. Casey told her he would, but asked her to call him and make sure he was home before they drove that far out of the way. She got all upset that he wouldn't just drive over there for her. She was not going to call. She wanted him to go over and hope he was home. Casey had driven a lot of miles in the past four days and didn't feel like adding another thirty miles without a sure contact. Her sons both had cell phones, as did she. The chances of them answering, wherever they were, were great. It didn't seem like much to ask, but it was enough to make her mad and ruin the rest of the trip.

Casey thought it would be fun to take Vanna to the National Rodeo Finals in Las Vegas the first week in December. He couldn't see how that could create a problem.

It was nice weather going to Las Vegas. The roads were clear, so they made good time going down. Casey drove, most of the way. Vanna wanted to drive so he let her take the wheel while he took a short nap.

The Mirage complex was easy to find. Casey figured out how to get to the parking lot in back. There was one stop sign on the way back, in the parking area. There was little or no traffic crossing there so Casey looked both ways and went slowly through the intersection. In Pinedale there was seldom traffic on anything but the main road. The police seldom worried about an old horse trader slowly driving though an intersection.

"This isn't Pinedale. Do you want to get us killed. You drive like an old farmer," Vanna criticized him.

He knew he was in the wrong, but at ten miles an hour he couldn't see how that was going to get them killed. Vanna was always exaggerating.

It was warm in Las Vegas for December. They didn't even need a coat to walk around. They visited the commercial displays at the convention center and another pavilion without Casey getting them lost.

Vanna wanted to buy a lot of the things she saw, but Casey wasn't putting more money out for salt and pepper shakers and the like so Vanna bought them with her credit card. She had a couple of sacks full, then found some cow hide pillow cases for twenty-five dollars apiece so Casey bought the four she wanted.

Casey could see you could go broke fast if you let your wants run wild where there were no needs.

It wasn't hard for Casey to find the Mack Arena from the hotel. Their seats were in the lower section, behind the calf chutes. Still, the action from the rough stock was so far away Casey found himself watching the monitor. It showed the present time action and then a rerun, just like the televised football games. At that rate, Casey figured it would be just as well to stay in the hotel and watch it on television; but there was something to be said for the atmosphere of being there.

After the rodeo, it was challenging to find the car in the dark. It took quite a number of minutes before they got out of the parking area and onto the main street.

The motel was to the left of where they entered the main street on the strip. Casey knew he needed to turn left but every intersection said no left turns. He wondered how he was to get back to the left.

"We're going the wrong way. The hotel is behind us. Are you lost?" Vanna irritably advised him

"I just can't turn to the left. If I turn right and go around the block I will come back on a no left turn sign again," he told her.

"Try that anyway. We can cross the main drag and go a block or so until we find a street we can turn left on," Vanna instructed.

Casey wasn't enjoying driving in the heavy traffic, but he did what he was told. The first thing he knew they were in a big grove of small trees; then, finally, they came to an intersection where they could turn left. After awhile they finally got back on the main road to take them to the hotel.

Sure enough, he didn't come to a complete stop in the parking lot.

"Didn't you see that stop sign?" Vanna hollered. "You sure drive like you're from the sticks, and I don't like riding with you."

"Maybe you better drive tomorrow night. You seem to know just how to do it," Casey proposed.

Vanna was mad that night and the next day. So much for the thought that nothing could happen to ruin the trip.

That night Casey offered to let her drive, but she knew her limitations and just got in the passenger's side.

It was another fiasco getting back to the hotel and they both were at wits ends before they got back to the hotel. This time Casey stopped at the sign in the parking lot, but that didn't help. She was mad, and that's how she would stay until they arrived home.

Vanna had jerked Casey around so much that he felt like the old star gazer horse he saw at the steer roping. His rider had jerked on his mouth so often that he carried his head high just trying to take hold of the bit to lessen the pain from his rider's jerk.

Casey was feeling that same fear of being jerked. He could see in that horse's eyes the fear and pain he also was feeling. Could people see it in his eyes, too?

When winter came and the ski season was in gear, Casey got a pair of cross- country skis for Vanna and took her on an outing. She didn't like the cold and didn't trust him to teach her how to ski. It didn't take long until she was ready to turn around and head back to the truck. Going back was a little down hill. She had a hard time not falling down. She swore she wouldn't do that again. That's how all winter went. She didn't want to do anything outdoors. If you live in the Rocky Mountains, you need to find some way to enjoy the winter or it makes for a long winter, Casey thought.

Right from the first of the marriage, Vanna would get mad about something at least once a week. In a few minutes she would get over it and be pleasant again so Casey let it slip by. This went on week after week. Casey was losing interest in doing things with her and losing his feelings for her.

These conditions continued for another year. It wasn't getting any better. Vanna had just been a roommate for the past year. She spent many days in central Utah with her family or friends; Casey wasn't sure which. From the first of October to the last of December, she spent forty days in Utah doing who knows what.

In October Casey noticed two quilts his mother had given him were missing. He confronted Vanna about the missing quilts. She finally admitted to taking them down to her sister's home. Casey told her she had to bring them back.

In November Casey was looking through the tack room which he kept a yearly inventory on. He had accumulated six thousand dollars worth of tack over the years. Two bridles were missing. They were the two Vanna had used on Roany.

Vanna and he were the only ones with access to the locked tack room. He confronted Vanna with this loss. She admitted to taking them. She said he had given them to her. Casey told her she had to bring the bridles back too.

A day later Casey was lying down on the floor with his dog in front of the TV when Vanna came in the room cussing him for something. Casey started to get up but before he could, Vanna pushed him down and kicked him in the ribs. It would have been easy for Casey to react adversely. He had a father who showed him, by example, to treat women as ladies. He had always treated Vanna that way. Opening doors, holding coats and being kind was Casey's way with women.

When he got up from the floor, he took hold of her shoulders and held her until she quieted down. He shook his fist at her.

"Are you going to hit me?" she said.

"No, I will never hit you, but someone needs to," he said.

He knew right then the saying, "Fools rush in where wise men fear to tread" fit him. He really was the fool.

He remembered his dad telling him a story about a snake. His dad saw a snake that was cold and almost immobile so he picked it up and took it home. He put it close to the stove. He could see the snake was feeling better. It was enjoying being where it was warm. Once the snake was warm and feeling good, he picked it up to put it back outside. The snake bit him and he cussed the snake. Then his mother said, "Well, you knew what it was when you picked it up."

Casey had been told to watch out or he would get bit, but he really hadn't seen the fangs of the snake until he was bitten. He told himself he would be very careful not to bring a snake home again.

He now knew no one could really know another person's inner feelings or understand how one's previous experience and relationships could affect a new relationship. He thought he knew Vanna after talking to her many hours and seeing the sweet feeling she exhibited towards him. Was it all an act too?

Casey knew how endorphins and adrenaline worked on horses. Endorphins made them relax and adrenaline caused them to become hyper. Some trainers would put a twitch (chain around the upper lip) on a horse and twist it up tight. The tighter they twisted it, the more adrenaline it created.

By taking hold of the lip with a hand and putting a little pressure caused the horse to produce endorphins. You would see the eye relax and start to drop. The lip would get soft and relaxed.

It was easier to handle a relaxed horse than one that was tense. This was true with horses and he had been told it worked the same on people. Those who are angry at someone caused adrenaline to flow when they were confronted.

Casey had not experienced this because he really was not mad at Vanna. He really cared for her and wanted to stay married to the sweet person in Vanna, but he couldn't live with the dark side of her personality.

Right then he knew he had to get out of this relationship which was going down hill fast and costing him one thousand dollars a month, for no closeness.

She didn't know Casey had talked to her lawyer weeks before she had retained him. He had told Casey that if he could show his wife had not contributed anything monetarily to the marriage and all the money had come from funds he had before they were married, he could fight her getting much money. The lawyer told Casey that the pre-nuptial agreement was of little value because it wasn't recorded in Wyoming.

Casey believed Vanna would try to get the money stated in the pre-nuptial agreement, plus the common property so he got Vanna to sign off on the agreement. Vanna told Casey she wanted one hundred fifty thousand dollars plus for the divorce.

It was Christmas in two more days. Casey and Vanna had agreed to get a divorce but had not agreed on the amount she would receive. She decided to go down to her kin's place for the holidays. Casey had given her eight hundred dollars for Christmas even though they were getting the divorce.

He had also given Vanna's mother seven hundred dollars to help pay for repairs to her car because she dropped her comprehensive insurance and had an accident. She never even said thanks. He also had given Vanna's nephew five hundred dollars because he was ill and had bills to pay.

He gave Vanna another one hundred dollar check just to show his charity. She came up to him and gave him a big kiss. He was really surprised. It was the first in months.

He was going to give the church a donation for the poor so he stopped into the bank to check his balance. It was twelve hundred dollars less than he thought it should be. He asked the teller about the shortage.

The teller said, "Oh, your wife stopped in just before Christmas and cashed a one hundred dollar check. She tried to withdraw twelve hundred dollars out of your checking account, but we wouldn't do that because you had changed it so she could only withdraw money in case of your death."

The teller told him Vanna had told her, "Oh! That must be why he gave me this other check for twelve hundred dollars."

"I had the bank vice-president okay it, then cashed it," the teller said.

"Couldn't you see the checks weren't alike?" Casey asked.

The teller pulled the two checks and they compared them. They were quite close, but the "J" on Jim was more closed and wasn't tilted to the left. The "C" on Case was open and round.

"It is not easy to see this one is a forgery, but if you look close you can tell. She did a good job," the teller said. "By the way, she closed her checking account and money market account at the same time."

Casey could see she had cleaned most of the money out of his checking account and she had committed a felony in the process. That had jail time, if she was prosecuted. But he would not prosecute her because he wouldn't want her put in jail, regardless. Even though he had indisputable proof.

Vanna could see she couldn't get Casey's bank accounts, but she could get half of the value of the property and half its contents. She had been told that by the local attorney. He had told her she should get one hundred thirty thousand dollars. Vanna was making it miserable enough that Casey was ready to actually file for a divorce.

It wasn't long until Vanna got tired of waiting for Casey to file so she made an appointment with the lawyer, Todd Mills, whom she had talked to earlier.

Todd didn't recognize Casey from their previous meeting so he informed Casey that Vanna was entitled to one hundred thirty thousand dollars and half of the items bought since they were married.

Casey told him straight out he wouldn't give her more than eighty thousand dollars, a car and a few things in the house. That was twenty-five thousand dollars more than the pre-nuptial would have given her, but they had shocked him with the request for one hundred thirty thousand dollars. He said he would giver her eighty thousand dollars. He knew she only had fifty-five thousand dollars coming.

Todd had been elected District Attorney for the area and was going to take over that job the first of the year. He said he wouldn't handle a contested divorce so they would each have to obtain a lawyer in Jackson.

Casey asked Vanna who she had obtained for a lawyer. She wouldn't tell him. Casey had been told by a friend of a lawyer they had used so he called him and got an appointment.

The day came for his appointment. Vanna asked Casey who his lawyer was and he told her.

She blew up and said, "You cannot have him. He is in the same law firm as my lawyer."

Casey called his lawyer and was told that the first one to come in for an appointment was the one they would represent. That sounded good because he had the first appointment. When he got to Jackson, Casey was told Vanna had made such a stink over the phone about the situation that the lawyer she spoke to said he would have to take her case.

The lawyer Casey talked to had arranged for another firm to handle Casey's case. Ben Barnes was the lawyer Casey got. He seemed professional enough and told Casey he was offering Vanna more than he needed to. Casey informed him he wanted to be fair. He directed Ben to file for a divorce giving Vanna the eighty thousand dollars plus the roan horse she had been riding and a number of things in the house.

Casey informed his lawyer and the District Attorney that Vanna had pushed him down and kicked him in the side. His attorney told him to go in and report it to the sheriff the next day which was the twentieth of January.

Vanna finally got to talk to her lawyer, Aaron Smith, on

the nineteenth of January. She didn't get home until 10:30 P.M. and went right to bed.

The next morning, Casey got up and fed the horses before fixing breakfast as he had done since they were married. Once Vanna got up and came up from the basement bedroom where she had been sleeping as of late, Casey asked her what her lawyer said. Casey figured she hadn't got the answers she wanted to hear. Casey later heard from his lawyer that her lawyer had told her that she should accept the proposal they had made. It was better than she could get going through a judge. She was upset because she wanted the one hundred thirty thousand dollars.

While Casey was home alone the day before, he got looking around at what Vanna had already boxed up. The first thing he saw was a box of toys he had had as a kid. He had kept them for visitor's kids to play with. All the farm animals, trucks, trailers and other toys were missing.

He opened a big, Rubber-Maid tub she used for storage and there was a full tub full of Barbie and Ken dolls. His mind swept back to the missing 1959 Barbie doll. How easy it would have been to slip that doll into her purse. He never suspected her at the time. He didn't dream he had married a thief, but it was quickly becoming evident that he had. How could she live with her conscience. She had been taking things all through their marriage. Maybe she had stolen from others before him.

That morning Casey confronted Vanna about the missing toys. She started hollering that she didn't take them. They both went down stairs to look at the box the toys had been in. She kept shouting that she hadn't taken them. Casey kept saying there was only the two of them there and he hadn't done anything with them. It got so confrontational that Casey turned, left the storage room and then started up the stairs.

Vanna followed him up the stairway, still hollering, "I didn't take them."

Casey was saying, "You did take them."

As Casey made it to the third step, Vanna was leaning her head on his back. With her hands down at her sides, she used her shoulders and upper arms to hit his back and sides. Casey turned around and gave her a slight push on the shoulders. She stepped back two steps but soon was back pushing on his back and hitting him as he went up the stairs.

Casey kept walking up the stairs. Vanna kept hitting him from side to side to the top of the stairs. At the upper landing, Vanna pushed Casey into the hall corner and kept hitting him until he brought his hands up and pushed her back off him. She had hit him over twenty times. She stepped back two steps, then dropped down on one hand and one knee. With a smile on her face and a twinkle in her eye, she stood up and ran to call 911. Her adrenaline was showing.

It took about ten minutes for the sheriff and his deputy to arrive. The sheriff took Vanna into the front room and the deputy took Casey into the kitchen. Casey told the deputy just what had happened. Vanna was crying when the deputy and Casey walked back into the front room. Casey was shocked at the red on Vanna's neck and upper arms. She had no redness on the under side of her upper arms. Casey thought at first that she must have gone in the bathroom and rubbed herself with a wash rag to get that red. As he reflected more on the situation, he realized she had kept her hands to her side and hit him with her arms to bruise herself, not to hurt him. The sheriff had taken pictures of Vanna's bruises and redness. She told him she had her arm twisted and was pushed down, but she didn't know how her neck got red. She cried deeply for him to see. That was the first time she had cried about their relationship, or the divorce.

The sheriff looked at Casey with disdain. "I could put you in jail for this," he said.

"You've got to be kidding," Casey replied, realizing he only pushed her off him twice.

"I am going to put you in jail for this, " the sheriff said. He hadn't even heard Casey's side of the story or looked at Casey's back to see the bruising. He just told the deputy to cuff Casey.

"You've got to be kidding," Casey repeated as the deputy put the handcuffs on him.

Casey couldn't believe he had been that unfairly treated. He had only been in the front room for less than two minutes before he was handcuffed with his arms behind him and put in the police car.

In the Army Casey was trained to kill in hand to hand combat with knives and weapons. He was trained in boxing to hit hard and fast, but he also learned how to be hit and not lose his cool. That's what he was doing when Vanna hit him in the back and arms with her upper arms. He could have turned around and pushed her down the stairs. He could have even defended himself, but he didn't even do that. He would never hit a woman, even if she wasn't being a lady.

Casey realized the whole scenario had been staged from the bottom of the stairs to the phone call. She had been prepared to get a better position for the divorce. She didn't realize the sheriff would arrest Casey. She even asked the sheriff not to arrest Casey, but to no avail. Her endorphins were showing. She was really happy to see Casey in trouble. Casey could see that made her feel good. She had the upper hand.

It was Casey's intent to go to the sheriff that day and report Vanna's abuse. Ben said that way they could have her evicted from the house. Couldn't they see he had no incentive to abuse her then?

Casey knew saying "You've got to be kidding" to the sheriff upset him and made him lose his cool. His adrenaline was showing. Vanna could have stopped her aggression at any time coming up the stairs or on the landing because Casey was trying to get away from her. She outweighed him and had an advantage because she knew Casey wouldn't hit her.

Casey found out Vanna had told the sheriff he had twisted her arm and pushed her down. He could see that the evidence of her red, bruised arms and neck couldn't be made by twisting her arm and pushing her down. Any person with half a brain could see that. He knew he hadn't twisted her arm or pushed her down. He had only pushed her off of him twice.

At the courthouse, Casey was booked into jail. He had never been so humiliated. He was finger printed on five different pieces of paper, then had his mug shots taken. He was given an orange jumpsuit to put on.

There were three other prisoners in the jail. One had two felonies against him and another had been framed by the previous sheriff. The sheriff was going on trial for it, but this guy was still in jail. These characters used the f-word every other word they spoke. They were some rough characters for sure.

That afternoon Casey was arraigned. The judge read the charges and asked how Casey plead. He told the judge he was innocent and asked if he could say anything about the case. The judge told him this wasn't the time.

Casey asked if he could go out and feed the horses. The judge agreed but he was told he couldn't go to the house. That meant he would have to take his dog and live at his parent's ranch for a while.

Vanna brought three of her girl friends to see the show at the arraignment. They couldn't have realized how humiliated Casey was. They got a kick out of seeing Casey in leg irons, handcuffs and an orange jumpsuit. He was totally ashamed of the circumstances she had put him in. He never dreamed he would be in this situation. He had never hurt anyone undeserving in his life. He had given to the poor and tried to do services to those who needed help. Now he was tagged as a wife beater. He knew he wasn't, but no one else but Vanna knew he wasn't.

At least, the judge let him out of jail that evening on his

own recognizance. He called his father to come get him. Would he believe he was innocent? Could he explain? He went right out to feed the horses, got his dog and truck, then went back to his parent's ranch. It was going to be many days before he would be back in his house.

That night Casey lay in bed trying to go to sleep. There was no sleep, just thoughts of what he could have done different and what would happen now. The crime he was charged with carried a one year jail sentence. His lawyer had told him if he went to trial, he would be convicted because of all the bruising and redness on Vanna.

Over and over he thought about the situation he was in. Night after night there was no sleep. He was innocent but no one cared, and no one was going to help him. He also knew that he was worth more dead than alive to Vanna. She had two sons and he wouldn't put it past them to see that he was. From then on, he kept a spare loaded pistol with him.

The next day Casey decided to look for some negative actions in her previous relationships. Casey called some of his acquaintances in central Utah to get the phone numbers of her ex-husbands. He found out Vanna's first husband died during his second marriage, but her second husband still lived in the area. Casey obtained his number and called.

Upon reaching the ex-husband's wife, he explained his situation and asked if her husband had had any problems with Vanna.

She told him, "He has many stories of his problems with her."

Casey called back and talked to Vanna's ex-husband. He

told Casey about how Vanna took a hammer and beat the bedroom door down because he had locked her out. He said he had been told by a number of his friends she was sleeping around. He knew she was stepping out with a horse trader he had recently sold a horse to. Later he admitted that she had him thrown in jail too. She had taken much of his stuff when she left him. He warned Casey to watch out for that. Casey wasn't able to find the last name of her live-in husband after a number of calls.

It was only a few days before the judge ordered Casey not to even enter the corrals to feed the horses because Vanna had complained about him looking in the garage window. She didn't want Casey to see what she was packing or what she had taken to her girlfriend's home. This made it so she had to go out in the cold to feed and water the horses. She wasn't going to like that.

Casey couldn't keep his mind off the divorce and what Vanna had done to him. It even seemed good to take a sleigh out to feed cattle, even if it was thirty below zero when he left the barnyard. It had been just over forty below when he got up and stoked the pot-bellied stove at five o'clock that morning. The bunkhouse was a log, one room building with a two hole out house behind. You had to pee in a can or hold it. There was no walking out in the snow to the outhouse at that time of the morning.

After the embers were stoked up, Casey slipped back in bed and dozed for another hour. By then the bunkhouse had warmed up so it was pleasant to get up and get dressed. There was hot running water if you wanted to run to the house for it. It was easier to wait until after supper and bring a hot bucket of water from the main house and shave.

Casey fed when a feeder needed the day off or was sick. The feeders hired on to feed seven days a week, but sometimes they had to have a day off. With five feeders, it seemed like Casey was feeding as much as the hired feeders were.

The hay teams were kept in the corrals so they could be fed hay as soon as the hand were dressed, about 6:00 A.M. That gave them some time to eat before they were harnessed and hooked to the sleigh at 8:00 A.M.

There were so many separate feed yards to feed in. Each feeder took a team and sleigh by himself. Most of the horses knew voice commands so it wasn't necessary to drive them.

The horses had frost all over their muzzles. The hair on their backs was topped with frost. It was so cold that Casey took off his glove and held each bit in his hand until it warmed up. Then the bit could be placed in each horse's mouth. If he didn't do this, he knew the horse's tongue would freeze to the bit. That could be real painful and injure the tongue so the horse wouldn't accept a bit making him unfit for work.

Coming to the first gate, Casey jumped off the sleigh saying, "Whoa." He opened the gate and kissed to the team. They pulled the sleigh through the gate. Casey again said "Whoa" and the team stopped.

He remembered that big, bull moose that caused the team to bolt when Kim was driving. Today was uneventful. Casey stepped up on the sleigh and kissed the horses up to a slow trot to the hay stack yard.

It was quiet except for a few cows bawling for their

breakfast. It gave Casey time to think of the beauty of the snow and the dark maroon color on the willows. The cows had frost all over. They were down in the willows for shelter but had started up to the hard packed feed ground when they saw Casey coming.

Casey liked this life, but it was a lonely life. Each of the hands who fed in the winter was alone, even with a bunkhouse of men. It was a lot the same for Casey. When he had Scott as a partner, he was a little less lonely but still wasn't content. He knew there was more to life than that. Then Vanna left him more alone, even when they were living together.

Yes, Vanna and the divorce were always one thought away. He just couldn't get it off his mind and wondered if he ever would get over the feeling that she left him with.

"Whoa," Casey hollered as he came to the hay yard gate. He jumped down and opened the gate. With a kiss, the team pulled the sleigh up against the stack as Casey hollered "Whoa."

Using the hayfork, Casey climbed up on the stack and started pitching. The stack hadn't been snowed on since it was fed from the day before. It was a lot of work pitching a sleigh load of hay. Casey rested for a couple of minutes before finishing the load.

Once again Vanna's actions were on his mind. It used to be that he was quite content out here feeding. Now he couldn't find anything that would take his mind totally off his problems.

Climbing down from the stack, Casey shut the back gate, opened the front gate, and moved the team out of the stack yard. He closed the gate then climbed back on the sleigh. He kissed to the horses and started pitching hay off the sleigh. The cows were all around the sleigh with more coming up from the willows. To make a circle on the feed ground, Casey hollered "Gee" and the team turned to the left in a long circle.

The cows coming out of the willows fell in behind the sleigh until the whole feed ground was covered in cows eating hay. Casey hollered "Haw" and the team turned right and headed for the creek. Taking the ax down from the sleigh, Casey walked over to the creek and started chopping. This was one job that would take your mind off of your troubles. With each swing, the ax sprayed up ice chips. As he broke through to water, the chips were mixed with water. The water was all over Casey's legs, even up on his face. It was so cold that the water and chips froze on his clothes and his face as it hit.

Soon he had chopped three holes open for the cows. He was warm on the inside from the chopping, but cold as cold on his hands and face.

It was good his dad had bought six sets of canvas bib overalls and canvas coats. They were lined and warm. The water would freeze on them, but he would stay dry inside. All the feeders were wearing them.

Casey could remember when all he had was long handle underwear, Levi pants, and a lined Levi jacket. All he had for his feet were rubber overshoes over his boots. He wore a pair of leather gloves to cover his hands. He wore the top of a woman's nylon stocking over his head and down on his ears, under his cowboy hat, to keep his ears warm.

His Levis would freeze solid from the water that splashed on them. His hands had been frost bitten so many times. Even now his down-filled gloves, would get wet making his hands freeze. Many times his hands would get so frozen he would take his gloves off and put his hands on the pine pole bars on the sleigh to warm them up. That was the olden days, and now he was almost too warm from pitching and chopping.

The team pulled the sleigh on a slow trot that took him to the next field. There was one sleigh load to feed in the morning and two in the afternoon. That much pitching kept him in shape in the winter. It wasn't like the city folk that kind of hibernate in the winter putting on fat for next summer.

On the ranch there were three big meals a day and still no one got fat.

Almost every evening and all long waking night hours Casey was filled with the problems facing him and trying to figure how to react. Would it ever end?

The next day Casey spent trying to get a hold of his lawyer on the phone. It was phone tag all morning. In the afternoon he finally reached him. Every time he talked to him it cost another hundred dollars.

Ben informed him that in the pre-trial phone conversation in which Casey wasn't included, the two lawyers and the prosecuting attorney discussed Casey's case. Ben, Casey's lawyer, called Casey and told him Todd, the district attorney, said to settle the divorce amicably and he would drop the spousal abuse case against Casey. Todd told Ben he didn't think Casey was a wife beater.

Vanna's second husband wrote a letter to Casey stating the abuse and loss he had endured from Vanna through his marriage and divorce to her. Casey took the letter to Ben and Ben said it might be helpful if they went to trial, but other than that the letter didn't mean much.

It shows a pattern, Casey thought. He took the letter to Todd, but he was not interested in it. Casey could show a pattern and could show the charges did not fit the evidence (her bruising and redness). Why wouldn't anyone look at this and drop the charges? It wasn't the facts; it was the pressure the charges could hold over him Todd was interested in.

Casey had prepared a proposal for a trade-off settlement of the case against him and the forgery charges the bank could bring against Vanna. This would have made a level playing field for the divorce. Aaron, Vanna's lawyer, agreed this was a good step and so informed Vanna. Aaron advised her to talk to Todd and tell him the truth so they could get him to drop the charges against Casey. He knew Vanna could go to jail for some time.

She didn't get back to Aaron. Either she didn't say anything to get the charges dropped or Todd advised her not to because she could be charged with giving false statements.

Casey felt Todd advised her not to say anything because he had control over Casey. Casey asked Ben to have Todd dismissed from the case because of a conflict of interest. Todd had been Vanna's lawyer at first and still was advising her.

"Oh, Todd wouldn't do that," Ben said.

Casey told Ben, "All Vanna had to do was blink her big blue eyes at him and he would do what's best for her, regardless of who is innocent or guilty."

Shortly thereafter Casey went in to talk with Todd about the case. Todd told Casey to settle the divorce and he would drop the assault charges.

The next step Casey took was to go into the sheriff's office to ask him some questions. He asked the sheriff if he was going to twist someone's arm, where would he take hold of her. He said the hand and wrist. Casey asked if that would cause any bruising on the upper arms or neck. He said it wouldn't.

Casey asked him, if he were to push someone down, would that cause bruising on the upper arms or neck. The sheriff said it wouldn't.

Casey suggested that by Vanna laying her head and neck against his rough shirt, she rubbed it raw as they came up the stairs since she was swinging her arms against his sides where his belt and belt keeper were; and that could have caused the redness and bruising. The sheriff said it was possible.

Casey asked the sheriff to talk to Todd, the Prosecuting Attorney, about these statements, but Casey never knew if he did. How would it look if he arrested the wrong abuser?

Casey told Ben to make an offer of fifty five thousand dollars, the amount the pre-nuptial agreement would have given her, plus the roan horse and a black leather couch set. It must have shaken her up because she made an offer to let the judge decide.

After it had gone on long enough, Casey told Ben to offer her eighty thousand dollars flat with no horse or anything else. He knew he had better stay close to his pistol now.

Vanna's lawyer told her she should take it and run. She finally agreed but told Aaron she was still going to get the horse. Her lawyer told her, flat out, the money was all she was going to get. Vanna had seven days to pack up and get out.

CHAPTER 12

DIVORCE AND LIFE AFTER

—————————————— U ——————————————

On March 4th, Casey met with Ben in the courthouse for a pre-trial hearing before the judge. Ben had the divorce papers Vanna had signed ready for Casey to sign. This was the best deal he felt he was going to get unless he went on trial, and it was not clear how that would go despite his innocence.

The District Attorney had held the abuse charges over his head even when he felt Casey was innocent. As soon as Casey signed the divorce papers, Ben took them in another room and the judge signed the divorce decree. Todd dropped the abuse charges within two minutes and Casey was free. The fact he was charged would always remain on the books. Vanna had marked him as an arrested wife beater for the rest of his life. Vanna got away with two physical abuse attacks against Casey and one case of forgery which was never filed because Ben had written in the divorce papers that Casey could not file the charges for forgery. Ben slipped that in without telling Casey. Ben had planned to just send the signature page for Casey to sign so Casey wouldn't see what all was in the decree. Vanna had not signed when she was supposed to so Ben was running late getting the papers to Casey. This gave Casey a chance to read the whole thing.

Casey was planning to sue Todd for interfering in his

divorce. He felt Todd had been blackmailing him to settle the divorce amicably with Vanna once Vanna had him thrown in jail. However, a paragraph in the decree stated that Casey would give up his right to sue anyone because he had signed the decree stating that he wasn't coerced into signing the divorce. He knew he had been coerced and knew Todd had been advising Vanna from their first meeting until the final decision. Then it was like Ben said: "That's just the way these things are done. There is nothing wrong with it."

Vanna had given the sheriff Casey's pistol and holster that he kept by the bed. Casey asked him if he could get his pistol back after he had signed the divorce and Todd dropped the restraint charges. The sheriff told him he couldn't get it back until the restraint decree from the judge was lifted.

"You have a six month decree to stay 300 feet apart. When that is up, you can get your pistol back," the sheriff told him.

"Are you sure about that?" Casey asked the sheriff in a questioning tone.

"I'm the sheriff, ain't I? I should know," the sheriff bluntly stated.

Ben would know, Casey thought. Back up to the court office Casey went. Ben told him he could get the pistol as soon as the judge signed the restraint release.

At 5:00 P.M. Vanna was to be out of the house so Casey could get back in. He left from town at ten to five. Arriving a couple of minutes to five, Casey stopped in the road until the minute hand was straight up, then he drove in. It seemed great to be back in his house. Now he could feed his horses, and he and his dog had the house back too.

When Casey got back in his house he saw how much of his property Vanna had taken. Vanna even left a can of soda pop in the freezer, just for meanness. It had exploded all over everything. She had kicked the tack room door hard enough to tear the doorframe apart but still couldn't get in so she had a locksmith drill the lock out. Then she had him change the lock on the barn door so it had to be drilled out before Casey could get in to get hay for the horses.

It was five days of back and forth confrontation with the sheriff before Casey finally got his pistol back. The sheriff had done all he could to hold the gun but found out the six month restraint decree was just an agreement, between the two parties. He wasn't very pleasant when he handed the pistol and holster over to Casey.

It had been a long forty-two days since Vanna had Casey put in jail. His lawyer fee was over four thousand dollars. He hadn't known much about the judicial system. He now knew much more about the system and was not too proud to be a part of it. Ben had told Casey he didn't want to go on trial because he had seen the guilty go free and the innocent jailed on tainted evidence. The outcome also depended on how the jurors felt about the defendant. If they didn't like their looks or how they talked, they would vote accordingly. That just wasn't what Casey thought the system was like. The system was so old and entrenched that there was nothing Casey could do to right such a wrong. All he knew was that he didn't want to get crossways with it again.

Vanna had had two personalities and Casey didn't want to get involved with another woman with the same problem, but then how do you know? Vanna had shown him her better side for at least a month after they were married and then the problem came on, little by little. Casey just put up with it. At first, she would cut in on a conversation and take over the discussion. Then, she began using a demeaning tone when she talked to him. It soon got so she would even belittle him around his friends and in public. Why had he stayed with her so long he wondered?

There was no love after the first year. The affection had been killed little by little. For the next year and a-half there was an unsaid agreement that they would just live together and try not to rock the boat. There was no closeness or sexual relationship.

She had told him she didn't like the way he made love. He figured she had made love with enough men to know. She also had said she didn't like the looks of an uncircumcised man.

He told her "I'm not Jewish, but most likely you haven't noticed with the interest you've shown."

It was hard trying to make love to her because she showed so little interest. Therefore it was hard for him to be interested. One night he could see she wasn't concentrating on what they were doing so he asked her what she was thinking about.

"I'm trying to figure out what to put on the grocery

list," she told him.

Casey could see why she wasn't that interested in making love. She had never come to a climax while they were making love. Casey asked her about this. He didn't know if it was his fault or if she had some physiological or psychological reason.

She told Casey she had never come to a climax and didn't know how it felt. She was just tired of men trying to get her to. How could she enjoy the fulfillment of making love? Casey thought.

Casey knew she was saying these things to upset him. She wanted to hasten the divorce yet she hadn't complained at the time. However, she had been with enough men to know the difference. Casey had been with only one other woman.

Casey remembered special ordering boots. He had a hard time getting a pair to fit. They were either too small or too large yet he had to take them because he ordered them. He decided it was much better to try them on before he bought them. He had ordered one pair that was too narrow in the neck, and he had to use some baby powder to get them on. That's how Vanna was. He could give the wrong fitting boots away but it cost him eighty thousand dollars to give her away. She was a pair of boots that made a sore on his heel that just wouldn't heal.

Without sexual closeness, a marriage has a hard time being successful. There are cases, sometimes due to health, where a couple can no longer have that closeness but they can still be loving. Vanna had put those cases up to him.

She didn't need the sexual closeness. She just wanted to live as friends. Casey didn't want to go through the rest of his life being a sugar daddy for her. Since they were married, it had cost him one thousand dollars a month to support her. As their relationship was, he didn't lose anything but money with the divorce, and now he could save the monthly money. She said she didn't want a divorce, but she did everything to create an environment for a divorce.

Looking back to Kim's outlook on life, Casey felt there were still people that had good relationships. He hoped that out there somewhere was a lady he could enjoy. He wasn't in any hurry to go looking for one. He was going to work the spring on the ranch. Then he might compete in the summer and fall. He still loved his horses and the western life, but he was going to be much more selective if there was ever to be another woman in his life.

Wouldn't it be justice if Kim and Vanna got together? They both were from adjacent towns in central Utah. Casey didn't know who he would feel the sorriest for.

After a week of just trying to get back to a normal day, or at least a stable day, Casey started thinking about putting Todd up before the State Bar Association for interfering with his divorce. After communication with the Bar Association, Casey got all the official papers together. He wrote a synopsis of the entire set of events from the first time he talked to Todd through Todd dropping the charges against him.

The person Casey talked to at the Bar Association said it would take some time to settle this case because they already had so many cases before them concerning lawyers' unethical behavior. Casey set the problem in the back of his mind and got on with working the horses he had started breaking.

By the middle of April, Casey was riding the colts to gather and sort cattle. He had roped a lot of calves and drug them to the fire where they were branded, earmarked and the bulls castrated. The colts were working well and Casey was pleased with their progress.

It had been a rainy spring and most of the corrals were muddy. Casey's neighbor had two foals, one Paint and one buckskin, born the same day. The horses were standing out in the storm so Casey told his neighbor to put the mares and foals in a corral he had. The corral had a big open front shed so the horses could get out of the storm.

Within a few days, Casey started talking to the foals and rubbing them on their tail heads. Once the foals got used to being rubbed on the tail head and rump, they soon started pushing into Casey to see if one colt could get more attention than the other colt. It got to be a game with them seeing who could push the other out of the way by backing between Casey and the other foal.

Casey rubbed the two foals all over. He rubbed over their eyes and would cover one eye then the other eye. He rubbed their ears and heads as well as their backs and bellies. Soon the foals were at ease when he rubbed them all over. To get them to pick up their feet Casey rubbed the cords which ran down the back of their lower legs. He didn't try to pick up their legs but just wanted them to enjoy his hand rubbing their legs. Once they were completely comfortable with that, he started picking up each foot for just a second, then would set it back down. Soon he held the leg up a little longer. Next he used a hoof pick to clean the dirt out of their hooves. This was before he had ever haltered the foals.

Casey didn't have time to play with the foals when they were very young. He had to halter break them the old way. Using a broom with a rag wrapped around it, he rubbed it up and down the legs until they quit kicking. He then rubbed the colt's leg cords until they would pick up their feet without a fight.

Casey liked to get the foals used to him touching them before he put a halter on. That way they had less resistance to the halter and rope.

After the rain stopped for a week, Gene, Casey's neighbor, took the mare with the Paint horse colt back home, but Casey had him leave the buckskin filly and her mother in the corral. Casey continued working with the filly. He would put the halter rope around the filly's neck and control her, just a little, and then let her go. Soon he had the halter on and was able to control her head.

"Come here," Casey would say as he pulled her to the side. This took her off balance. To catch her balance, she had to move her feet to keep from falling. In three days, he was leading her around the corral like an old broke horse.

Within a couple of weeks, Gene had a mare due to foal again. Gene was out of town the day his wife noticed the mare lying down and getting up. She did this quite a few times. Realizing the mare was having trouble, Gene's wife called Casey for help.

Casey hurried right over. He found the mare lying down pushing the foal out a little, then standing up and the foal would go back in. The next time she laid down, Casey took a hold of the foal's feet and pulled on them a little. This time the mare stayed down and kept pushing. This was the mare's first foal and she wasn't sure what was happening.

Soon the legs were out and Casey could see the head between the upper legs. He reached out and opened the placenta around the foal's mouth and nose. Now it could get air even if it took a little more time to come out.

Casey pulled a little more with each push the mare made. Soon the head and shoulders were out. Then the belly and hips slipped out. The mare didn't lie there long. She got up and in that move, the umbilical cord broke and the foal was free. Soon the foal was up and shaking.

What a great feeling it was for Casey to see the mare and foal both doing well. Casey had had many mares give birth in the years he had raised horses, but he had never been there when they foaled. His vet had told him that humans caused more problems than they solved when a mare was giving birth. Casey knew this was true, but he also knew of a lot of calves he had pulled from first time heifers. He had lost a few cows and calves because the calf's head was just too big for a two year old heifer. He had been breeding Angus bulls to his young heifers so the calves would be a little smaller and the cows would have less problems calving.

The mare and foal were moved to Casey's corral so they wouldn't have all the other mares, without foals, trying to get too close to the new baby.

CHAPTER 13

LEGAL MANURE

---U---

The Bar Association sent Casey's charges to Todd, the district attorney, to refute.

Once they received his rebuttal, the Association forwarded it to Casey to comment on.

Todd's rebuttal was very weak and the comments he made were refuted by Casey. One interesting comment Todd made was that he wasn't Vanna's lawyer. He had just helped her out and never charged her. Casey's lawyer charged him every time he called, even if it was just for two minutes. Ben always put down fifteen or thirty minutes for charging purposes.

Casey sent his rebuttal back to the Association stating that Todd had said to him, "I will send Vanna a letter telling her I am no longer her lawyer now I am the County Attorney." That was good enough for Casey to support that argument.

Casey was encouraged. He had a strong case so he checked around to find a lawyer who would prosecute his case against Todd. After calling a number of lawyers and being turned down, Casey finally found one who would meet with him. This lawyer, Ron Kerby, had been Past President of the Bar Association.

Casey sent all of his materials to Ron and, in a couple of weeks received a call from the lawyer's secretary who set up an appointment the next week.

It was a great shock to Casey to be told that Todd had not broken the law or even the ethics with the exception of giving

Vanna advice and meeting with Vanna and Casey as her lawyer after he had previously talked to Casey. Ron Kerby told Casey, "That's just the way lawyers function so they can settle cases out of court by pressuring one of the parties to give into the other's demands. Plea bargains are handled that way all the time," he told Casey.

Casey knew he didn't like how lawyers functioned in order to get by the letter of the law regardless of the intent of the law. Yet Ron was telling him he didn't think he would do any good suing Todd. He said Casey would have to pay, up front, for him to take the case no matter what the outcome.

With this judgement in front of him, Casey decided to call the Bar Association and drop the case against Todd. Casey was an honest, up-standing person and he didn't find the lawyers that he had dealt with to measure up to that level. He was going to be a better man than they were.

Shortly thereafter, Casey received a letter stating all the facts of the case and spelling out the pros and cons, but in the end the Bar Association stated Casey had withdrawn the case and no actions would be taken.

Casey was sure he had been wronged by a number of lawyers. Vanna had gotten away with two attacks of physical abuse and one case of forgery, then she got paid eighty thousand dollars. She never returned the things she had taken or repaired the damages to the house and tack room.

Months after the divorce, Casey was still discovering other things that were missing. Would it ever stop? Vanna even had the neighbor photograph the redness on her neck and arms. With these pictures, she could support her argument that Casey had abused her. There was nothing Casey could do to counter these stories she was telling her friends and family.

CHAPTER 14

SELLING A PAINT

Getting ready for a horse sale takes a lot of riding; it also takes a lot of grooming. Casey had a Paint, a six year old gelding, that had the body of a Quarter Horse with a great disposition. He had been riding the Paint for two years and was ready to sell.

Casey thought this horse might top the sale so he stated it in the sale catalog under sale horse description. Some sellers might take offense to this remark, but Casey believed it.

At the sale his horse was penned right next to the bleachers around the sale ring. All the noise might have upset other horses but this horse didn't worry about the noise or people.

Casey rode his horse around the rodeo grounds so people could see how quietly he worked. He was surprised not many buyers had talked to him about his horse. The sale had high selling horses and low sales. You couldn't always tell why one horse sold so high and another went low.

There was a working ranch horse competition for those owners who wanted to compete for monetary prizes in addition to showing off their horses. Casey hadn't believed the judge was correct in his judging. There were riders riding with two hands and other riders with one hand. They were all being judged equally. They shouldn't have been.   For this reason, Casey didn't see any advantage in competing in the event.

Casey was getting a little worried about how his horse would sell because no one had approached him about the horse. Usually people would want to watch the horses travel or watch how they rode out.

When the three year old palomino mare that won the working ranch horse competition came through the sale ring, the pedigree reader really tried to sell her on the fact she had won the event. The auctioneer worked hard to get the buyers to bid, then stopped so the pedigree man could talk her up. They got the bid up to seventy two hundred dollars by offering to give the bidder one hundred dollars just to bid once more. Finally they got all they could get out of her.

There were 168 horses in the sale. It was mid-afternoon before Casey's number was called for. His horse was number 82. The sale management had set the opening bid for each horse at $900. As Casey's horse entered the ring, an old rancher told the ring man closest to him to open the bidding with his bid of four thousand dollars. The ring man checked twice with the man to make sure he was hearing right.

When he told the auctioneer the opening bid was four thousand dollars, the auctioneer didn't believe what he was hearing so he took a minute to clarify the bid. The auctioneer thought it was Casey's set up bid. Casey had topped this sale a number of years earlier. He had also twice topped another sale this auctioneer worked.

The bidding started at four thousand dollars and the rancher who started the bidding took him to fifty eight hundred dollars, then stopped. There were still two bidders in. That's all it takes, two bidders to make a run. The two bidders went right up to seven thousand one hundred dollars without the auctioneer even stopping to talk the horse up. A different pedigree man had been put on the stand and he didn't try to say anything. As soon as the bidding stopped at seventy one hundred dollars the auctioneer said "Sold!" He didn't want Casey's horse being the high selling horse because he hadn't even competed in the working ranch horse competition. They were trying to market the sale as a working ranch horse sale.

Casey had planned to pull the bridle off and ride the horse bareback to show how well he was broke. When the auctioneer said "Sold," that was the end of the bidding and he had no chance to show his horse off more.

Casey wasn't upset that the horse didn't bring more money because he would have been happy with five thousand dollars. What he was upset about was the fact that the horse sold himself for seventy one hundred dollars without any help from the auctioneer or the pedigree man. Another factor was that the sales management gave a one thousand dollar bonus for the high selling horse. Casey had no doubt in his mind that the second bidder would have bid again if he had been prodded a little. All it would have taken was two bids and he would have had the high selling horse.

One consolation was that they decided to give Casey three hundred dollars for the high selling gelding. This was only because Casey called the sale manager the next day and told him he thought he got a bad deal. The manager was working as the pedigree man when the palomino mare went through the ring. He was also a retired judge in the county. Casey appealed to his honesty as a judge.

Casey was asked to pose for a picture with the buyer of his horse. The high selling palomino mare wasn't photographed. Casey and his horse's picture were in a number of papers and magazines as the top gelding in the sale. This pleased Casey. It is important to let people know you have good horses which bring good prices.

CHAPTER 15

KIM HANGS UP HIS SPURS

When Casey arrived home, he found a message on his phone answering machine. It was from a friend of Kim's. Kim had been diagnosed with progressive cancer of the brain. He had been fighting it for over a year and now he was in the hospital in the last days of life and wanted to see Casey.

The next day Casey left for Salt Lake City to see Kim. As he drove, he reminisced about his relatively short acquaintance with Kim. He knew they weren't much alike, yet in a way they were alike because they both wanted to live the Western life and be their own boss. An eight to five job didn't fit either one of them.

Casey called and found out Kim had gotten married to a sweet, innocent gal. They had one child. Kim had named him Casey. Casey thought Wow! What an honor!

When he arrived at the hospital, he went right to the room he was told Kim was in. What do you say to a man who is dying? He had never been in this position before. He hoped he could keep his composure and say the right things.

Kim was so excited to see Casey. Even with all the medication he was on for pain, he was able to give Casey a big smile and a hearty, "Hello, Partner."

Casey asked how he was doing and Kim said "Okay, compared to the alternative". Kim was more interested in reminiscing about their experiences together.

After they had talked for over an hour, Kim showed signs of tiring. Casey knew he had better let him rest now. Kim asked him to go meet his wife and son. Casey was planning on that anyway. He was planning on staying over and coming back the next day.

"I sure hope you feel better, Kim," Casey said.

"I'm dying, Casey. I won't feel better. I'm just trying to handle it until I die," Kim answered.

That took Casey back. He just didn't know what to say.

"I'll see you tomorrow, Kim. Try to get some rest and we will talk more then," Casey replied.

Casey went out into the waiting area where he met Kim's wife and year old son. Casey introduced himself to her. As she picked her son up, she said, "This is Casey. Kim wanted you to see him. He is a good boy and Kim is the best father and husband we could have."

What had caused the change in Kim? Casey wondered. What more of an honor could Kim have given Casey? Had he made an impact on Kim? He hoped so.

Casey spent a few minutes talking to Kim's wife and playing with his namesake. She was quite bitter about Kim being taken away from her. She felt she had too little time with him and now she was going to have to raise a son alone.

Casey left the hospital and found a motel for the night. The next morning Casey got breakfast and went shopping for a gift for Kim's son. Of course, he asked instructions to the nearest western wear store. There he found a little pair of jeans. The clerk helped him find a shirt which would fit a yearling. He got these wrapped and headed for the hospital.

Again he went right to Kim's room. As he entered the room, he saw the bed was made and the room was neat and clean. Kim was not there. A nurse was passing by and Casey asked her where Kim had been taken.

"I'm sorry. He passed away last evening," she informed him.

That meant Kim hadn't lived long after he left last night. He felt bad Kim was gone, but Casey was sure glad he came when he did.

Casey called Kim's father and asked when the funeral was but found there would be no funeral. They were going to have Kim cremated and scatter his ashes in the hills above his home.

Kim's wife had already left for her parent's home in California. Casey never got another chance to see her and little Casey. He was able to get an address for her and sent the little outfit he had bought

On the drive home, Casey went over in his mind how tentative life is. He knew he should appreciate the fact he had his health and what he needed to live comfortably on. He knew that was more than a lot of people had.

SONNY

Casey no more than got home when Gene, his neighbor, came over and told him he was having trouble catching a two year old filly he had just bought.

"Casey, I put the filly in the round pen and ran her around until she was tired but I still couldn't get up to her. I'm getting nowhere with the 'Horse Whisperer' method. What should I do?" Gene asked.

Casey grabbed his rope and rode back over to Gene's place. The filly was still in the round corral. She looked wild-eyed as Casey entered the pen.

Building a loop, Casey let the filly move around the round pen once. Then up and out went the houlahand loop, settling over her head and onto her neck.

Many horsemen would have walked in swinging the rope over their heads like a steer roper. This would cause the horse to panic and run around the pen. Casey used the houlahand because it only went around his head once and it sailed out quiet and easy. Most horses didn't see it coming.

Hank, the ranch foreman, had taught him how to throw the loop when he was young. Casey found it the most useful loop in his repertoire. He thought it was sad it was a lost art in roping.

Rather than letting her keep running, Casey cut her off as she tried to get by him. He hadn't pulled the rope tight yet. He wanted to settle her down and let the adrenaline stop flowing. He tried to maintain eye contact all of the time he was cutting her off.

Soon she stopped and stood still. Now Casey pulled the slack out of his rope and started to step closer. As she tried to turn away from him, he pulled on the rope to keep eye contact. Each time she tried to pull away, Casey held tight, then pulled easy on the rope saying, "Come here."

Soon Casey had worked his way up the rope and had his hand on the horse's neck. Petting her and talking to her, he moved to having his hands all over her head, covering her eyes as she relaxed and gave to his touch.

As Casey pulled to the side, he told her, "Come here." Soon she was giving to his pull. She was also munching her lips. This indicated she was giving in and relaxing. It was time to put the halter on her. Working slowly around her neck, he slipped the halter strap under her throat with his left hand, then took hold of it with his right hand over the top of her neck. The nose hole was flipped out catching her nose. With little objection from the filly, Casey buckled up the halter.

He worked the rope over her head and dropped it. Now, he had a hold of the halter rope. Pulling to one side with the "Come here" command, the filly was soon coming to the pull. Within ten minutes, the filly was following Casey all over the pen.

"Here is your halter broke horse," Casey said.

Gene couldn't believe the change in the filly. Casey couldn't believe it either. He was lucky enough to catch her with the first loop. Next she gave to his touch and voice. It doesn't always happen that easily.

While Casey was at Gene's place, he noticed a two year old gelding Gene had raised.

"What's this gelding?" Casey asked.

"Oh, that's one I raised out of the big buckskin mare and the buckskin stud over there," Gene replied.

Casey was impressed with the shape of the gelding and his grullo color.

"This two year old is a half brother to the buckskin filly you've been playing with," Gene commented.

"What would you take for this colt?" Casey asked.

"Oh, I would sell you both the filly and this colt for eighteen hundred dollars," Gene said.

Casey thought of the sale he had made that spring on the Paint horse. This horse could top the sale, too, if he was broke well. He knew he didn't need the filly because he had a policy of not buying female horses to sell. But this was too good a buy to pass up.

"I'll take them both at that price," Casey told Gene.

The two year old was barely halter broke and had little gentling or grooming.

Casey picked up the gelding the next day. He looked as good the second day as the first.

Now what should I name these two horses, Casey

pondered. Looking at the papers of the filly, he found the name of a stallion he was well acquainted with. He had owned a son of this stallion. He had trained the gelding for two years and had topped a big sale. The stallion's name was Opies News Flash so he decided to call the filly Opie.

The gelding had a predecessor on the top side with SUN in his name and another on the bottom with SON in his name so Casey decided Sonny would fit this colt fine. He had a lot of horses he called Son, only that was short for S.O.B. A number of horses had earned the name.

Casey had to start right from lesson one with Sonny. He worked on the halter training and the massage lessons. Soon Sonny was trusting Casey to rub him all over, cover his eyes and rub his ears. He wasn't that good with his feet so Casey had to start rubbing the cords in the back of Sonny's legs.

The colt was big enough to ride so Casey started sacking him out and saddling him up. It wasn't long before he was bridled and pulled from side to side to learn to give to pressure.

Sonny was learning so fast and working quiet and relaxed. Now it was time to drive the colt. Casey ran a line on each side and to the rear of Sonny. He pulled on the left rein and Sonny walked to the left side. Casey stayed directly behind Sonny so he didn't get pressure on both reins at the same time.

Casey was starting to get worried about Sonny. He was just learning so fast and so easy. On the next lesson,

Casey started stopping him and backing him up.

On the third day of driving Sonny, Casey was getting tired of walking. He put a white five gallon bucket on the ground next to Sonny and stepped up on it. This way he wouldn't startle the colt by jumping for his stirrup. Sonny was not concerned so Casey stepped right on. Sonny wasn't sure what was happening but didn't let it upset him. He was responding to Casey's pull on each rein to turn, stop and back.

The old timers say you might get away with stealing a ride on a horse once or twice but the third time is the one to watch out for, yet Casey's third ride was better than the first two. Day after day, Sonny got better. Casey put shoes on him and was riding out of the round pen on the fifth ride.

Casey put Sonny through an obstacle course he had set up for the colts. Sonny never reacted like other colts. He just walked over the logs, backed through the "L", smelled the 4x8 sheet of plywood, then walked over it the short way then the long way. Casey had a rope tied onto a log for the colts to pull. Sonny looked at the rope as Casey got off and put the rope on the horn. Casey stepped back on and asked Sonny to back up. Usually the colts would get upset when the log moved towards them as they backed up. Sonny never worried about it, but he did keep his eyes on it. Casey turned him around and let him pull the log behind him. This didn't bother him either.

This was the easiest horse he had ever broke. This one should really sell for a good price, Casey thought. He started throwing the rope off Sonny while he was following cattle. Sonny acted cowy so Casey figured someone could make a rope horse with some age and seasoning on him.

A PHONE CALL

U

It had been two weeks since Kim had passed away. Casey was still going over in his mind what he might have said to comfort Kim. How do you comfort someone who is dying and knows it is close? Casey just couldn't think of what he might have said to comfort him. It was a fact of life and Kim had accepted it but Casey hadn't.

Who might be interested in knowing Kim had died? Casey wondered. He was sure Kim's wife hadn't known about Susie May. Casey wondered if Susie would even care, but they had been quite close for over a year.

Casey thought after three years Susie might still be following the circuit running the barrels. He had no idea where she might be with rodeos being held all through the early summer months.

His first idea was to put an ad in the Professional Rodeo Association magazine. She would surely be reading that to get the standing of all the top competitors in the rodeo. He called the number which was on his last copy. He had made an ad which might catch her eye.

Susie May, Kim is now riding bulls in the sky. Call (307) 814-0106 for more information.

Now, who else might be interested? Casey only knew one other person who had known Kim. That was Samantha.

She really wasn't that well acquainted with Kim but then would most likely want to know anyway.

Casey called the Denver hospital to see if he could catch her at work. With his luck, she was not working. He couldn't get her number from the hospital so he left a message for her to call him. Now all he could do was wait for that call.

The first call was from a cowboy who had known Kim and Susie May. "I don't know if Susie will be interested in Kim's passing. She is married to a dentist who did some dental work for her. She doesn't chase cans anymore and she has a new baby, I heard," the cowboy said.

"I'm sure sorry Kim died," the cowboy told Casey. "Kim was a wild guy and lived life to the fullest. I imagine there will be a lot of gals who will miss him."

Casey broke in, "You didn't know the Kim who just died. He was an honorable family man who loved his wife and son. I know this doesn't sound like the Kim you knew but that's the man he was when he died. That's the one I will remember."

"Well, that's great," the cowboy said. "I'll spread the word around that he has passed away and I'll tell what a great dad he was."

Casey pondered the idea of calling the number the cowboy had given him for Susie. He decided it would be best to let her live her new life without being reminded of another time and person.

It wasn't long before Samantha called. Casey told her about Kim's wife and baby and how happy they had been until they learned Kim had brain cancer.

Samantha was quietly crying as Casey explained the situation Kim had been in just waiting to die. She was a very open and loving person. She had a hard time with her patients dying in the hospital too.

"How are you doing, Casey?" Samantha asked.

"Oh, I'm getting by," Casey told her. "I got married and it didn't work out so I'm alone now." My ex-wife got married, for the fifth time the other day and I hope she's happier than she was with me. It only took her seven months to find another sugar daddy."

"That's strange. I got married, but my marriage didn't work out either. It was really hard on me, but I couldn't live with a person who turned cold," she told him.

"I'm not pressed with work right now. How are you set? Do you have some leave time built up?" Casey asked.

"I do have some leave built up," she replied.

"Why don't I send you a ticket to fly into Salt Lake City and I'll pick you up there?" Casey questioned.

"That sounds like a great idea. I can take off next Monday," she said.

She gave Casey her address and telephone number so he could get the flight worked out and send her the ticket.

What a great stroke of luck. She was single and had time to come see him. Casey was on top of the moon. He wondered what she would be like out of the hospital setting. Casey didn't remember seeing a single lady since he got divorced. It was like they were all holed up. He knew there must be a number of them in Pinedale and the surrounding towns. He knew it would be easier to get acquainted if Sam lived closer, but sometimes that isn't possible. Casey knew Samantha to some degree but was not sure how she would like the cold in the winter and the ever present mosquitoes and horse flies in the summer. The wet meadows were prime breeding grounds for the pests.

Casey could hardly wait for Monday to come. He cleaned the house and yard and got a few flowers to plant in the front yard. He had planted a lot of pine trees and they were getting some size to them.

He had filled the house with paintings of cowboys and horses. Over the fireplace was a big painting of a Hereford bull. What was she going to think of his decorating?

What would his Australian Shepherd dog think of Sam? Sissy was a one-man dog and didn't take to very many people. Even his folks couldn't pet her for the first year Casey had her. She was a real friend for Casey. Every time he moved, she was up and ready to go with him. She loved to go working cows or just riding in the open country which Casey did quite often.

CHAPTER 18
SAM VISITS WYOMING

∪

On Sunday, Casey drove to Salt Lake City. It was about a four hour drive. He had washed the truck and vacuumed it all out so he could make a good impression. After being with Kim and his family and hearing about Susie's change, he knew people did not have to be as entrenched as he thought they were. He was willing to try to change and adapt his life to someone else's desires, but how was he going to feel if someone wanted to change his house and his way of life. But Samantha was coming for a visit, not a marriage.

It took all his concentration to follow the signs to get to the short-term parking.

As he parked, he looked around to see the section letter and number he was in so he could find the truck when he came back. It was D5 so he had a little walk to get to the terminal. Once in the terminal, he found himself on a big belt which was moving him into the center of the terminal.

What a waste of energy, he thought. That was probably why people in cities were so over-weight. They had no activities. Then the government tries to convince people they need to reduce their weight while building more facilities which reduce human energy output.

You just didn't see people on ranches who were obese.

There was too much work feeding cattle, breaking horses, fencing and putting up hay to gain weight. However, he had seen all the equipment advertised in the magazines which did the work for the rancher. They got to sit in a big tractor cab which was air conditioned and heated with stereo sound all around them.

Casey was sure glad they would never be able to make a machine to break and train horses. There would always be a job for him.

Remembering back to the last time he was at the airport, he had been able to meet his friend at the gate where he came in. Now he couldn't leave the foyer of the terminal. He would just have to wait for Samantha to come to him.

The flight from Denver was on time so she would be coming soon.

Casey was getting anxious to see her. He thought he knew what she looked like, but now he wasn't sure.

With his hat on, he stood out in the big entry center. He was watching the gate exit area, but he didn't see her come down the escalator.

"Casey, here I am," he heard someone shout. It was Samantha. He waved at her and quickly walked to her. She looked different without her white nurse's uniform. She looked more mature and yet was still very attractive. She was still slim and neat. Her work kept her slim too. With her makeup on, she looked more beautiful than the gals on TV. Her light skin was set off with the short black hair and pretty blue-gray eyes. The red lipstick topped everything off.

"Oh! It's good to see you again," Casey said as he gave her a hug.

"Well, you haven't changed at all," Sam said. "You're still that cowboy I remember."

"Look at you, in jeans and roper cowboy boots. You look like you'll fit right in at the ranch," Casey told her.

"My Dad, a truck driver, wears boots. He bought me these for Christmas, last year," Sam said.

"You look so cute, but not just as I remember. You have cut your hair and have more make up on which brightens your countenance. You look great," Casey assured her.

"Why, thanks for the compliment, but it isn't my looks I want you to see; it's me as a person outside of the hospital. I hope you get to know the real me," Sam informed him.

Sam pointed out her two suitcases so Casey could grab them as they went around the luggage return carousel. Then they went up the escalator to the big belt that took them to the parking area.

"Now if I can remember the area where I parked the truck," Casey said, almost to himself. "D5 was where I parked, I think."

Sure enough, his truck was right where he parked it.

"Boy is this truck clean and shiny! Is your house this clean, too?" Sam asked.

"Not always, but I do try to keep things shaped up," Casey replied.

Jumping up in the truck while Casey held the door was no big effort to this agile lady. Casey was sure this was going to be a fun five days.

They never stopped talking during the whole trip to his ranch. It was the most enjoyable conversation he had had, but he remembered how Vanna and he had also enjoyed each other when they drove to a horse sale. He couldn't let his loneliness sway his reasoning this time.

"There is my place on the left," Casey informed her.

"You do have a lot of trees. That round area in front with those two horses is nice," Sam said.

"Yeah, I always wanted a place where I could sit on the porch and watch the horses as the sun was going down in the west. I have seen a lot of beautiful sunsets here, but I have had no one to share them with," Casey said.

"Well, we will have to enjoy some of those sunsets together," Sam responded. "This is really a nice house and it's so clean. Who do you get to clean it?" Sam asked.

"I clean it myself. It helps to kill time for me. It's better than just sitting around in the evening doing nothing," Casey said.

"You really have decorated the house Western. The pictures and hand-made tables and lamps are especially attractive. I haven't ever seen anything like them. The Navajo rugs really add color to the rooms," Sam said. "I could really enjoy this place."

"You'll have five days to try it out," Casey said.

They were both tired from the long ride so Casey took

Sam's luggage to the spare bedroom where she could freshen up. Within a few minutes, Sam came into the front room and sprawled out on the couch.

"This is sure a comfortable couch. I could go to sleep here. The sun is coming in through the window and it is so pleasant," Sam said.

"Go ahead, sleep for a while and I will go feed. I need to let my dog out of her pen too," Casey informed her.

"Not on your life. I'm going with you. I want to see your dog, horses and the rest of your facilities," Sam responded.

"This is Sissy," Casey told Sam as he let the dog out of her pen.

"Isn't that a big house for one dog?" Sam questioned.

"Well, you see, Vanna had two dogs and I had one so I built a dog house with three bedrooms, a front room, plus a loft. Vanna asked why I had made them such a nice doghouse. I told her she had a nice house so the dogs deserved a nice home, too," Casey said. "Now Sissy lives in it alone. She's kinda like me so we spend a lot of time together to help reduce the loneliness."

Sissy came out of the pen wagging her tail and rubbing her head against Casey's legs.

"I can see she really loves you. You can tell by the loving look in her eyes when she looks at you," Sam said.

"Yes, she is my dog. She wouldn't let anyone else even touch her for a year after I got her. She had been mistreated and then ran wild for a while before the dog catcher used a tranquilizer dart to catch her. She was in the pound when I got her. She bonded quickly to me and has been my dog ever since," Casey responded.

"Do you think she will let me pet her?" Sam asked.

"She didn't like Vanna and she wouldn't mind her at all. You'll just have to talk to her and let her read you," Casey said.

Sam approached Sissy with slow, cautious movements. Sam spoke to Sissy softly in a gentle voice. Sissy didn't move back behind Casey as she usually did with strangers. Sam spoke her name. Sissy came a step toward her and waited for Sam's hand to touch her.

"She is a good judge of character so I would say you're a good character. Look how she is looking up into your eyes with that loving look she gives me. You must be someone she wants to know, and that goes for me too," Casey said.

They fed the horses and put some cat food out.

"I only feed the cats a little bit. They are mousers and I don't want them to get used to being kept. They need to remember they have to keep the mice out of the sheds and the voles out of the pasture. They do a good job too," Casey said.

That evening, they ate some hot dogs and veggies. It was too late to cook much. Then they went to bed and Casey tried to get some sleep. It was about as bad as the sleep after a big cow cutting. He went over the day's activities time and again. He kept jerking to get the door or do something to help Sam. He was really into reliving the day with Sam.

The next morning, Casey was up early. He shaved and dressed. The chores didn't take long and Casey was soon back in the house. He could hear Sam up and around.

He had always cooked breakfast for himself, then for Vanna, and now for himself again. This breakfast would be a pleasure to fix. He got the side pork out and started to fry that, then he put some French toast on. About then Sam came in the kitchen looking bright and shiny.

"What can I do to help?" she asked.

"You can set the table and pour some juice if you want," Casey told her.

Breakfast was an important meal for Casey. It started the day off right. The side pork gave him the protein he needed for a good day's work.

"Well, how was that breakfast?" Casey asked.

"That was really great, but I'm stuffed. I'm not used to eating a big breakfast," she returned.

"We have a big day ahead so you better be full. We're going to move some cows today if that is okay with you," he said.

"That sounds fun, but you don't know if I can get on a horse, let alone ride one," Sam said.

They went out to the corral and Casey caught a couple of horses. He saddled and bridled them.

"This one is very gentle. All you have to do is keep one leg on each side and your mind in the middle," Casey told her.

He was ready to help her on as she walked up to the horse. One bounce and her boot was in the stirrup. Another bounce and she was setting square in the middle of the saddle.

"Where did you learn to get on like that?" Casey said surprised.

"I didn't tell you my Dad had a horse as well as boots. He let me ride it quite often so I got comfortable riding," she said.

The day was really a success. Casey didn't have to babysit Sam, and he enjoyed seeing her have fun chasing after the calves which kept trying to drop back.

As they unsaddled, Casey could see how calm and comfortable Sam was around her horse. She knew to undo the back cinch before she undid the front. "You sure did a good job with that horse today," he said.

"Why, thank you, that is a real compliment coming from a pro like you," she replied.

"When I was real young, my Dad always mounted me with horses that knew more than I did and they were gentle. They taught me more about working cows than a human could have. If you learn to trust a good horse, he won't let you down," Casey said.

That night he took her down to the ranch for a barbecue and to meet his folks. She fit right in and had a relaxed look in her face. Maybe she could fit into this type of life, Casey thought.

The next night Casey barbecued some steaks at home

while Samantha set the table and got the odds and ends ready. After supper they snuggled down and talked while listening to old cowboy songs.

"These songs sound a lot better to my ears than what they call country music. I can't understand half of the words some of those would-be cowboys sing. These songs are easy to listen to and you can even think while you're listening," he said.

The next day they saddled up the four-wheelers and loaded them in the horse trailer for a ride in the hills.

"I thought you would have one of those fancy horse trailers like I saw at the horse show this winter," Sam stated.

"Here on the ranch, we have too many things to use a trailer for to have one with all the dividers and a fancy tack room. We load all kinds of things in these trailers, and the horses haul fine in them," Casey replied.

"Anyway, I'm not one to spend money for things just so people can see you're a spend thrift. Money comes too hard on a ranch."

Samantha could relate to that because a truck driver doesn't bring home a lot of money either. Her family had to make money stretch all the time growing up. She didn't get overpaid being a nurse and she had to put in long hours to get that.

Sam handled the four-wheelers as well as she did the horse. Now if she could ski, he'd buy her some.

"Have you ever skied before, Sam?" Casey asked.

"I took ski lessons a few times, but it cost so much I couldn't afford to keep it up," Samantha replied.

"The type of skiing I like doesn't cost much of anything once you have the skis," Casey said. "Cross-country skiing is what I like because it is quiet and the scenery is great. Snowmobiling is so noisy and you have to keep your eyes on the trail or you could run into something. Cross-country skiing is so peaceful and is less work than walking. I will have to teach you how. I'm sure you would catch right on."

"I like the winter on clear, sunny days. It looks so clean and bright. I just bundle up. I'm sure I would enjoy it," she said.

That was sure a lot different than Vanna. Vanna hated the winter and didn't want to step out of the house, let alone go skiing. She didn't even give cross-country skiing a chance. She had spent the winter reading and doing word puzzles.

How enjoyable it was to be with someone who could laugh and have fun just being out in the good fresh air.

The days went by fast and before he knew it, he had shown Sam all the pretty lakes and had ridden some fun rides through the desert. It was time to take her back to Salt Lake City to catch the plane home. They had talked about everything so they didn't talk much on the drive back to Salt Lake. They both were doing a lot of thinking.

Casey knew five days wasn't enough to be sure Sam would fit in. He wondered too if they could be happy together, but he had sure been happy for these five days.

When they got Sam checked in at the desk, she only had fifteen minutes before boarding. Casey knew he wanted her, but he wasn't sure what she wanted. Only time would tell.

"I sure hate to leave," Sam said. "I have had so much fun and enjoyed being with you. You're quite the host. I'm sure going to miss those good breakfasts you've been cooking."

"Come back and I will cook you some more. It's not much fun just cooking for myself. I have enjoyed having you here. It has really brightened my days. Now you just have to come back," Casey said.

Giving her a big hug and kiss, Casey walked Sam to the security station where he would have to leave her. He could see she had wet eyes. The emotion was welling up in his eyes too.

Squeezing her tight, he knew this wasn't going to be the end of their relationship.

CHAPTER 19

A TRUE COMPANION

U

Casey had a lot of work to do to get the calves branded before they would be turned out on the desert or taken to the upper ranch for the summer. He used the colts he had been breaking. It was good for their training. He had to pay all his attention to put the colts where he needed them to rope the calves and drag them to the fire. With two sets of calf holders, he had to hurry to catch and drag another calf to the fire.

There each calf was thrown to the ground and held by two cowboys on foot. One held the front leg in a bind while the other sat behind the calf and pushed it's lower leg forward with his foot while pulling the upper leg to stretch the calf out. It was then branded, ear marked, vaccinated and castrated if it was a bull calf. This job was hard work and could get a little dangerous when a mother cow came running to help her bawling calf, but there were always plenty of cowboys up for the job.

Cowboys gave the calves a week to recuperate before moving them to the upper ranch. This was a long, slow drive because there were so many young calves to push along.

Casey always rode the point of the herd or one wing and let the hired hands bring up the drag. When riding on the wing or side of the herd, Casey would build a loop in his rope and tie a string around the hondo and rope so it wouldn't close. He then roped calf after calf and they would just step out of the loop. This was good practice for the colts, but it also improved Casey's heeling loop. It also took his mind off his loneliness and his desire for Samantha. He called her once a week and talked to her for an hour at a time. It really brightened his disposition all that week.

Sam had such a sweet, friendly voice and she was so interesting to talk to that Casey had a hard time not calling her more often.

To keep himself busy, Casey had worked on a pair of chink chaps for Sam. They were made of soft leather that looked like elk hide but was really cow hide tanned to look like elk. This made a little thicker hide which would hold up well and shed the rain instead of soaking it up.

Casey carved pictures of horses on the chap's belt. He put fancy conchos on the sides and carved Sam's name on the back of the belt. These chaps were extra special.

Casey wrote Samantha a letter and put it in the box with the chaps. Within a week, he got a call from Sam.

"Yes, I will," came the voice on the other end. Your proposal was very sweet and the chaps look great. I can't wait to wear them when I get back there," she said.

"I'm so glad. I didn't know if you would say 'yes', or just tell me you didn't know enough about me," Casey responded.

"Oh, I think you are a very nice man. I would have no fear living with you. You have shown me that in everything you have said and done," Sam said.

"If you're sure, then give the hospital two weeks notice

and we will get married the last week in July if that's okay with you," Casey suggested.

"That sounds great. I won't have too much to plan before the wedding. We can get married here in Denver so Mom and Dad can be there," Sam informed him.

"Then we can have a reception back at the ranch," Casey said.

They worked out a few more details and agreed to talk again soon. Casey was really excited about having Sam for his wife. The last week in July was only three weeks away. He decided not to ask a lot of people to the reception. His close friends and parents would sure like to come, he thought.

The work had slowed down in July to mainly fencing and repairing equipment for haying the first of August. He realized he was going to be busy haying so he had better take Sam on a good honeymoon the last of July.

Time passed quickly and soon he was on his way to Denver. The flight was quite exciting. He had not flown much and when he did it had been good weather. This time the thunder clouds were thick and there was lightning flashing off in the distance.

The pilot came on the intercom and welcomed the passengers to the flight. He told them the air was turbulent so they were to keep their seat belts on.

Casey had never had any trouble throwing up on flights so he wasn't worried. All at once the seat fell out from under him, then came back fast and hard. He was glad he had his seat belt on. As he looked out the window, he could see the lightning flashing from one cloud to another. It was very close to the plane. Casey wondered what would happen if it did hit the plane, but he sure didn't want to find out on this flight.

As they landed, he was happy to get out of that turbulent air. He was thanking the Lord for a safe trip. After Kim, he knew life could end at any time from any cause. He wanted time to spend with Samantha.

Grabbing Sam, Casey held her close for some time. That flight had increased his awareness of life. He was so glad to hold her again and feel her warm body next to his.

Casey met Sam's parents and found them almost as pleasant to be around as Sam was. They were warm, friendly and easy to talk to. They asked him about the ranch and what he was going to do for the future.

The future was something Casey hadn't dwelt on. He liked competing in rodeos, but he wasn't going to ask Sam to follow him around the circuit. That just left building up his ranch which would complement his dad's. He was going to inherit half of or more of his parent's ranch. He had one sister who had left home and got married young. She didn't like the ranch life and now lived in Casper, Wyoming. She worked in an office, as did her husband. Casey knew they wouldn't be coming home. He could buy her part of the inheritance from her. One day the big ranch would be his.

The wedding went well and the next afternoon they were on a plane heading back to Salt Lake City. The flight was smooth and they chatted the whole hour coming back. It was late when they got back to Salt Lake City, so they got a motel and enjoyed the night.

Casey lay awake quite a while after Samantha fell asleep. He thought about his life and the interactions with people in his life. He had met a lot of nice people, but he had never felt like he had an inward bond which took care of his need to not feel alone. Even with Vanna, there was a separation between them. He wondered if he would ever feel satisfied with a closeness which didn't leave him with that loner feeling. He hoped Samantha and he could find that true fulfilling love. Maybe he had been a loner for so long he wouldn't be able to give himself totally and completely. Vanna had really put a kink in his emotions. He didn't want to give his heart just to have it spit on. He really felt he could find that open complete feeling of love with Sam. She was so loving and giving of herself and her feelings.

After breakfast, they started on the trip to the ranch. Casey put a cassette of old western songs in the tape player. He had heard them so many times he sang along. Samantha snuggled up against him, holding his right hand tightly.

"You're too beautiful to be a Sam. Your eyes always sparkle and your black hair is set off with that pretty white skin. You look more beautiful the more I know you," Casey told her.

"Well, my dad wanted a boy so he gave me a boy's nick name. He made me into a tomboy when I was young. We did a lot of man things. I enjoyed it and those experiences made me more ready for you. I'm your wife, but I also want to be your partner," Sam said.

"You're the best partner I've ever had and you will always be my partner."

"Are you happy, Sam?" Casey asked.

"Oh, I am so happy. More so than I have ever been. I never felt this way with my first husband. He just wasn't open and warm. I tried to make up for it but he always seemed cool and aloof. He would shut me out of our relationship. We would go days not talking to each other. I have felt close to you right from the first. You are so warm and open. This will give us a foundation where we can build a warm and open love which will grow with everything we do together," she said to him.

Casey figured Sam had had enough old western music so he put on some contemporary western music he knew she enjoyed. He had a hard time making out what some of the present western singers were saying. He just listened to the music and enjoyed the tempo.

It was a long ride back to the ranch. They were both tired so Casey let the ranch hand he had feeding for him take care of the night feeding.

"I will give you money to buy some special items of furniture and decorations so you will feel more like this is your home, too," Casey told her. He was going to make her feel at home as much as he could. He wanted her to be happy in her new home.

Casey's parents had set up a nice reception at the ranch. It was well attended and everything went smoothly. He was so glad that she had enjoyed his parents and them her. Vanna had at first, then turned cold. He didn't want that to happen to them again.

They took off the next day for a honeymoon to Jackson

and then were going on to Cody and Yellowstone Park. Sam had never been to this area of the west so she had much new country to enjoy in the few days they had to spend.

Casey mentally compared the honeymoon with Vanna to Samantha. It was apparent there was so much more openness and love. There were no disagreements or frigid feelings. It was so nice to be able to enjoy the openness and tender feelings of love.

Back at the ranch, the hay crew was getting the equipment in working shape and repairing harnesses he never finished. The draft horses used for haying were summered at the upper ranch on Horse Creek. Casey asked a couple of the old cowboy hands to go with him to the upper ranch to bring the horses down. They loaded the three saddled horses in the truck and a driver drove them to the upper ranch, twenty five miles away.

Once they reached the upper ranch, they unloaded their horses and started off for the highest hills on the ranch. The cows utilized the meadows and the lower hills. The horses liked the high hills where there was a wind or at least a breeze to blow the flies away. The mosquitoes and horse flies were so prevalent at the lower altitudes that the horses seldom came down.

Once they found the horses, they headed them down to the corrals by the homestead. They knew the way so all the cowboys had to do was follow them down. In the corral, Casey rode among the forty-some head of horses and cut out the ones they would not use because they were too young or retirees. Once a horse had worked well for years and was old and weakened by age, they were retired until they died. Casey's dad always told him he had an obligation to take care of them because of the good service they had given to the ranch.

The gate out of the corral onto the road was opened and the race was on. The draft horses knew their way home. All the cowboys had to do was try to keep up with them and open four gates. The horses would stop at each one, then hard trot and lope to the next.

There was an afternoon storm building fast. The lightning was striking up on the high hills and moving closer. Casey knew lightning could strike ten miles in front of the storm. They had traveled about ten miles when Casey decided to pull into a ranch at the next gate.

This rancher had a herd of greyhound dogs for hunting coyotes. There were ducks, geese, peacocks, chickens and turkeys all over the place. The horses scattered them all as they came into the barnyard and on into the corral.

Jake, the owner, came out and looked at the sky.

"Put your saddle horses in the barn and come on in," he said. "Looks like a dangerous lightning storm. You could get hit real easy moving with that herd of horses. You made a good decision to pull up."

"I really appreciate your letting us hole up for an hour or so. It looks like it will move by quite fast," Casey told him.

"Come on in. We're just setting down to dinner. There is plenty. You like buffalo?" Jake asked.

"I haven't tried buffalo before, Jake, but I could sure try

it." Casey said.

After washing up, they sat down to a big meal. The buffalo was heavily seasoned and so was the gravy. Casey and his hands were hungry so they chowed down.

Jake tried to tell about his coyote chases every time he got a chance. He spun stories for over an hour.

Casey looked out the window and could see the storm had gone on.

"It looks like it's time to move those horses down to the ranch," Casey informed Jake. "Thanks for the food and letting us pull in."

Within a half an hour, Casey's' buffalo was trying to get out of his stomach and into his mouth. He had had a little light heart burn before, but this wasn't little or light. With each step of the trotting horse, his chest felt like it would explode and he felt like he was burning up.

With this problem to fight all the way home, Casey had one of the worst rides he had ever had. He was sure glad he chose not to bring Sam on this ride. She would have been soured on riding quick.

The next morning Casey still had the taste of buffalo in his mouth, but the real burning had subsided.

In the haying seasons, the crew worked every day it didn't rain and so did Casey and his dad. It was long hours and hard work. Casey mowed hay with a team everyday. That meant he had to sharpen two seven foot mower blades each night so he could start out with a sharp blade, then change to a sharpened blade at noon.

When the mowers got ahead of the stackers, Casey would go up on the stack and help the stackers speed up the work.

This workload resulted in a tired, hungry husband each night. Sam didn't have enough to do. She had planted more flowers and some small trees, but still she got lonesome not having anyone to talk to. She discussed with Casey the possibility of trying to get a job at the hospital. She knew there was always a need for nurses.

Casey was not completely happy with her going to work, but he realized she didn't have much of a life with him gone so much.

"Okay, you get a job, but how about just taking a part time job? I won't be this tied up for much longer, then we can go do some fun things. You can ride with me gathering cattle," Casey suggested.

After a couple of reference calls by the hospital administrator, Sam had a job. She did find it rewarding to be productive and having people to interact with.

Casey could realize a little more why he felt alone so much. All he had to talk to was two horses, and even they only showed their rear ends to him. He enjoyed training saddle horses and did have more interaction with them, but still he was lonely. He had to find more time to spend with Sam.

After the first snow storm, the haying was over. The hay wouldn't dry enough to stack. The meadows that were not hayed would be used to feed cattle that were brought home for the winter.

The next ranch chore was to bring the cows and calves home for the winter. The calves had grown to 450 to 500 pounds. They would be able to travel faster than when they had traveled up as babies. It only took one drive to bring the cattle down from the Horse Creek Ranch, but the horses took another trip later. Casey knew that was more a race than a drive.

Samantha made the cattle drive. She had started to bond with ol' Rock, a good old cow horse that had never had a chance to bond with anyone and was enjoying her attention. She had bonded with Casey's dog and even the cat liked her. Casey knew he had bonded with her. He had never felt so at ease in his life. The loneliness had subsided and it was replaced with a deep love for Samantha.

The cattle, which were on the forest grazing areas, would come out of the mountains as the snow and cold drove them down. When they got down to the ranch's altitude, there was a fence across a narrow strip of land that stopped the cattle from going farther south. It was the cowboy's job to go out to this drift fence, separate their cattle from the herd and take them to the ranch. This collection had to be made every day until all the cattle drifted down from the forest.

Three days after a big storm, there would be a large number of cattle waiting to be sorted and returned to their owners. Some days there could be up to one thousand head standing by the fence waiting to be sorted.

It was Sam and another cowboy's job to hold Casey and his dad's cattle in a nearby spot as they were sorted from the herd. She liked riding ol' Rock because he knew how to hold the herd. He was always alert to catch cows trying to get back to the big herd.

It was Casey's job to sort out their cattle and push them towards their smaller herd. This was similar to cutting cattle in the cow cutting competitions. In cutting, the cutter cuts the cow out and then two turn-back men push the cow back towards the cutter. This causes the cutting horse to have to work hard to keep the cow from getting back to the herd.

In sorting on the ranch, the person sorting has his horse move the selected cow out of the herd towards the hold. There were no turn-back men. The cowboy on the outer edge of the main herd picked up the cow that was cut out and moved it to the hold herd, making sorting easier and quicker than cutting competitions.

Once in a while the brand on a cow grew over or was not burned deep enough. The cowboys had to rope the head and heels of the cow so the brand could be clipped for a more accurate reading. Casey enjoyed these incidents because he got to practice his roping. Sam was impressed with Casey's sorting and roping. She knew he was a real cowboy.

The colts needed work too so Casey often selected a colt to ride on the drift collection. He wasn't able to cut cows out of the herd on the colts, but there were five other ranchers with cowboys sorting their cattle. They would sort out Casey's cattle as they sorted their own. Once the cattle going to the upper six ranches were sorted out, the gate was opened to let the rest of the cattle go south to the next drift fence. Usually, they separated out about half of the main herd before they sent the rest south.

CHAPTER 20
BACK FROM THE LIGHT

♡

The morning was clear and cold as they saddled up. It had been fair weather the past few days so the expectation was for few cattle to be at the drift. Ol' Rock was always mellow, even on cold days. Sam never had to worry about him except when he turned quickly to head a cow. Then she had to grab the horn as it went by so she could go the same direction.

Casey had saddled up one of the colts Kim had started. He was snorty when Casey saddled him. As he pulled the front cinch up the back of the saddle came up. The colt had a hump in his back. Casey hadn't even stepped him off and tightened the cinch yet. This was why Casey wanted to break the horses with kindness. They were much less apt to come apart, when it was cold or when they got in a tight situation.

Casey stepped the colt off a few steps, tightened his cinch and walked him another couple of steps before stepping on. As he swung his right leg over the saddle, he could feel the colt bunch up. He had no more than sat down when the horse exploded.

Now horses are broke at two or three years old in the city but on the ranch they were grown out slower. They weren't broke until they were four or five. This colt was five and totally mature. Casey had twelve hundred pounds of dynamite under him. This colt could buck with power and quickness.

As the horse bucked, he put a little spin into the jumps.

Casey had all he could handle. He was glad he was in the round corral where the colt couldn't get a run at the buck.

Casey wasn't spurring. He was just trying to ride the colt. There was no eight second buzzer like in the rodeo where a pickup man comes and takes you off. This kind of bronc riding was win or lose and there was no time restriction. Sometimes they would buck for over a few minutes which seemed more like an hour. This was one of those times. Casey had a hold of the saddle horn. Watching every movement the horse made, Casey just tried to stay in the middle.

Soon the colt's head came up. Casey drove him towards the fence and turned left, then right, making him give to the rein. These colts Kim had started just weren't handling like the ones he started. He knew why he broke colts the way he did.

Casey thought when a horse starts to buck, riding him wasn't something you learn to do by reading a book or having someone tell you how. It's something that comes with practice and a natural ability to maintain your balance. It only took losing your balance for just a second and you end up eating dirt. Yet sometimes you rode by the seat of your pants and somehow you kept coming down in the right place. You don't know how you rode the horse because you weren't in rhythm from the first jump. Who knew how or why you stayed on? Casey had experience with each of these situations and hadn't been thrown more that a handful of times. He rode lots of colts that bucked with him. Casey remembered one time vividly. Scott and he were breaking colts and riding them in the summer when the flies were bad. It seemed the only time to ride was after dark. This night was light as day with a big, full moon. They had ridden out on the desert pasture where the flies weren't as bad. Casey was loping his colt out when a covey of sage grouse flew up right under his colt. The colt went to bucking. Casey was making a good ride when he felt the colt somersaulting on him. At least that's what it felt like. Instead, the colt had bucked so long and hard and sucked back when he hit hard. The saddle and blanket came right over his neck and head. Casey lit with the saddle still between his legs. He even saw the blanket flop down beside him. That time he never got hurt. He resaddled the colt and continued the ride. Casey had been lucky that way. He had been rolled on a number of times. A number of horses had reared over backwards and caught his leg under them. All these left sore spots that ached more over time, but he wasn't all busted up.

One time he was riding with some friends in the hills. His friend offered him some candy so he took the package and started to remove a few pieces. The colt he was on wasn't mean or unruly, but the sound of the plastic sack set him off. The colt hit three times and the next jump he sucked back. Casey lit right in front of him on his feet, with the reins between his legs and the candy was still in his hand. One of the closest riders looked down from his horse and said, "You sure are agile for your age."

Casey hadn't done a thing. The colt had done it all by himself. That's how life on horses had gone for him. A lot of excitement but little hurt.

Sam, Casey and two cowboys rode out of the corral and over the bridge into the pasture. They put the horses on a hard trot to take some of the high off them. Casey's colt had no more than broke into a trot, when he stampeded on a run. This was what Casey hated. He knew the colt would run, then stop hard, and light into bucking. Casey pushed his feet forward and sat back in the saddle. All at once, the colt hit hard and started bucking. Casey sat up and rode him out. He didn't have as hard of a ride this time, but the hard stop almost unseated him.

"I almost lost him, when he hit hard and started bucking. I thought I was going over his head, but somehow I stayed with him. He just came up under me. It was like I had a sky hook that kept me on top of him. The rest of the ride was easy after making that first hit and jump. "Maybe I haven't lost my touch, after all," Casey expressed.

Sam was very impressed with Casey's ability to ride a bronc. She had been to a number of rodeos and hadn't seen a horse buck any harder than this one. She had a feeling of danger even though Casey was good. He could still get hurt.

It was a four mile ride to the drift fence. They didn't waste any time because the other cowboys started sorting early.

Sam held their cattle. The two cowboys helped pick up cattle as they were sorted and pushed them into the owner's herds. Every once in a while Sam's horse would see a cow trying to get out of the hold herd, and he would swing fast to stop the quitter. She had had bruises on her thighs ever since they started riding the drift. She couldn't imagine the bruising Casey must have on his.

Casey worked the colt by picking up sorted cattle and was getting along well. He decided to go into the main herd and sort out one of their cows. He got into the herd and the cows started pushing against the colt. The pressure was more than the colt could handle. Down went his head and up came his butt. Casey was into another hurricane only this time there were cows all around him. All the cowboys were watching. Casey didn't touch the horn this time. He rode the colt through the herd, scattering cattle left and right. Casey could feel the horse starting to give up so he decided to give him a spanking. He overed and undered him with his reins. This caused the colt to buck more and harder, but soon he gave up and up came his head. He had had enough.

With shouts and hoots, the cowboys showed their

appreciation for a good ride. These cowboys knew what it was like to ride a horse to a stand still and not just eight seconds. Most of them were top hands. Casey appreciated their approval.

Soon, they had their cattle sorted out and were on the trail to the ranch. It was open desert for the first three miles, then there was a dirt road up to the ranch. The cattle were moving fine, but Casey could see a gate open into a pasture up ahead. He knew he would lose some cattle there if he didn't ride up and post his horse at the open gate.

He broke the colt into a lope along the barrow pit. The colt was tired so he was quiet loping up past the cattle on the road. As he passed the head cow, he felt the front end of the colt drop out from under him. He saw the ground coming up in his face. He realized the colt was coming over in a somersault on top of him. He felt pressure on his chest as his head hit the ground. The colt rolled over him and stood up. Casey didn't move.

The colt was standing in the open gate so the cowboys quickly pushed the herd past the colt. Sam pushed along the side of the herd to get to Casey. She had not seen any movement from Casey as she rode up.

Jumping off Rock, Sam ran to Casey. She started checking his vital signs. Right off she could see he was not breathing. She checked his pulse and found none. Was he dead, she thought. He couldn't be. She needed him so much. Quickly she started CPR.

The cowboys rode up and asked what they could do.

"Ride to the next ranch, call for an ambulance and tell

them it is a 'stat' situation," she said.

She kept the CPR going, checking to see if he had a pulse. As she pressed on his sternum, she could feel a weakness on one side. He must have broken ribs on that side, she thought, so she put her pressure just below the sternum. It seemed like it took the ambulance forever to get to them. She had found a very weak pulse but could not see him breathing.

Once in the ambulance, the medical personnel put the defibrillator on his chest and shocked his body. There was no response so they did it again. Air started to be taken in. He was possibly alive, Sam thought. Could he keep breathing, even shallowly, on oxygen, she wondered.

At the hospital Casey was put in an emergency room. There were doctors checking him on each side. No one said how he was doing, but Sam could see from the machines he was hooked up to that he wasn't stable.

"We're losing him," one of the doctors said. "Get the defibrillator."

Again, they shocked him twice before the life line on the machine showed a movement, even though it was small.

One day after another slipped by without much change. Sam knew that Casey might have brain damage because of the poor supply of oxygen he had had. They wouldn't let her work as his nurse because she was too close to the situation. All she could do was sit and watch him try to breathe.

Casey had a concussion, broken ribs and a punctured lung. The saddle horn had hit his upper ribs and his head had hit the ground. He had taken a real hard blow to both areas.

Sam drove out to the sight of the accident. She looked around to try to figure out why the colt would have somersaulted just loping along. He wasn't doing anything wrong.

After looking up and down the barrow pit, she finally found the spot where the sod and dirt was dug up. She found an old wood culvert in front of the open gate. At the end of the culvert where the horse's feet went down, Sam found a hole the water had washed out where the grass was as high as the surrounding grass. Casey couldn't have seen the hole nor could the colt. Sam remembered seeing the colt's front end drop and his rear end go over, pushing his body down on Casey.

Driving back to the hospital, Sam was thinking how lucky Casey had been not to have been killed on the spot. Yet he almost was, and the outcome was still not confirmed. She wondered if he would live, and what medical problems he might have.

As Sam opened the hallway door the nurse on duty came running towards her.

"Samantha, your husband woke up about an hour ago. He seems like he is mentally okay," the nurse informed her.

Sam's eyes brightened and a big smile came over her face as she ran to Casey's room.

Casey had a smile on his face as their eyes met. He couldn't move much more than his hand, but he was holding that out to her.

Without a word, Samantha dropped down over him and gave him a big hug. She was shaking with excitement. This was the answer to her prayers.

"It's okay, honey," Casey consoled her. "I am just about with it. They tell me I have been lying here for over a week. That's the biggest rest I have ever had."

"I am so glad you came back to me. I thought you were going to leave me forever," Sam said.

"You mention that and I remember something. Kim said to tell you 'Hi,'" he said.

"What do you mean Kim said to tell me 'Hi?'"

"I'll tell you what happened. I remember the colt's front end going down and then nothing. Soon I was looking down at you checking me over then everything went dark and a bright light shown above me. I felt myself moving towards the light. The next thing I remembered was seeing Kim. He came to me and told me he had been keeping track of me for some time now. He said he had to pick who he was going to watch over and he had picked his wife, his child and me. Can you believe that?"

"He said I was not broken up so much that I couldn't come back. He reminded me that his tumor had eaten away his brain so he didn't have that choice."

"Did you want to come back?" she asked.

"Very much so," he told her. "In all my life I have never been so at ease or felt so loved from someone. I am glad I had the opportunity to give you the love I had stored in me. Yes! I wanted to come back.

"Why didn't you come back sooner? I have been going crazy worrying about you."

"I'm sorry I troubled you so, but Kim was very lonesome

waiting for his family even though time passes very fast for him. He told me he had finally found love and had become at peace with himself and with his family. He wasn't lonely anymore. Leaving them had been very hard, but being able to watch over them had helped."

"Kim apologized for not doing a better job of breaking that colt. He asked me if I could remember when I about lost my seat as the colt ran and bucked. He said he had pulled me back in balance with the colt allowing me to ride him out. If he hadn't have done that, he said I would have got dumped."

"Why didn't he save you from that fall then?" Sam asked.

"I asked him about that too. He said he wasn't able to see the future; and before he saw the colt go down, I was under him. He said he did pound on my chest a few times before you got to me. If he hadn't, he said I probably wouldn't have breathed again."

"He said not to depend on him. I needed to take fewer chances so I would be able to stay with you."

"I have told you that a number of times, but you just keep putting yourself in danger," she told him.

"You know, now as I think of it I remember seeing horses there, but no one was riding them. We were able to move from place to place as fast as the horses. I thought this would sure save the wear on my rear end. Does that mean I won't be training horses up there?" Casey kidded her, but the thought puzzled him.

"By the way, Kim said he would keep an eye on you too," Casey told her.

"You just tell him to stay out of our bedroom. I can keep you safe there," Sam chided.

"You know, my mother told me my grandmother had taken the death of my uncle Ted very hard. He was only sixteen years old and it was Easter. He went out alone to catch a stallion in the field. The horse would let him get right up to him then would turn and run. Ted got a rope and when the horse let him get up close to him, he threw a loop over his head. The

horse turned and ran. Ted had let a tail of the rope get behind him. As the slack went out of the rope, the tail whipped up around his shoulder and neck. The first jerk must have broken his neck, but the horse drug him through five barbed wire fences before someone got a gun and shot the horse.

"Grandmother was so distraught she couldn't sleep. About a week after his death, Ted came back and stood at the foot of her bed. He told her he was fine and she shouldn't worry about him. She felt so much better knowing he was moving on and wasn't just a body in a hole in the ground. I took the story with a grain of salt, but not any more. I saw Kim and talked to him. He was as real as you are. I want you to know, you have an angel watching out for you here. I'm sure you're going to have a long life," Casey said.

The week of unconsciousness had let his ribs rest and heal without stress or pain. His concussion had cleared and his headaches were quite mild. Within two days he was up walking and eating solid foods. Another day and he was getting into the truck and riding home with Sam. He was so happy he had Samantha to go home with. He really felt at ease with life. He realized how fortunate he was to have found Samantha and built a love with her that left him fulfilled and not lonesome anymore.

THE END

ABOUT THE AUTHOR

U

J'Wayne "Mac" McArthur is the retired Horsemanship Program Director at Utah State University in Logan, Utah. He taught horsemanship, colt breaking, horse judging, packing, roping, shoeing, and cowboy crafts.

While working for the U.S. Department of Agriculture, Economic Research Service after graduate school, Mac published research on many of the western states at USDA Washington, D.C. Upon joining the faculty at Utah State University, he continued publishing at that institution as well as New Mexico State University and University of Utah.

Mac has published many articles in national horse magazines including the Western Horseman, Quarter Horse Journal, Hoofs and Horns and The Appaloosa News. He has written weekly horse columns in the Herald Journal in Logan, Utah and the The Post Register in Idaho Falls, Idaho. He had columns in The Farmer Stockman magazine in Utah, Idaho, Washington, Oregon, Montana, and Nevada, as well as The Grainews magazine in Winnepeg, Canada for a number of years.

In 1990, Mac was named "Teacher of the Year" at Utah State University. At the age of 73, Mac was inducted into the 2009 Salmon Select Sale Hall of Fame in Salmon, Idaho as All-Time Champion and presented a beautiful

Montana Silversmith buckle in recognition for buying the most horses over the years and selling top priced horses at the sale. Mac has owned over 1,000 head of horses and produced his own Broke Horse Sale for 13 years prior to retiring.

OTHER BOOKS BY
J'WAYNE "MAC" MCARTHUR

Training For Western Horse and Rider. *A 343 page guide to owning, riding and training the western horse with over 300 photographs and drawings. 6th Edition.*

The Cowboy Life in Short Stories and Poems. *A 126 page story and poem book to make you laugh and cry. 3rd Edition.*

The Friendly Beast, The First Domestication of the Horse. *A 43 page children's book about the domestication of the horse.*

Two Trails, One Great Adventure. *A 61 page book, a story for pet lovers.*

Spokane, 1889 Kentucky Derby Winner from Montana. *A 118 page book about a Montana horse that won the Kentucky Derby and set a race track speed record.*

Ollikut: War Chief of the Nez Perce. *A 260 page historical fiction about the plight of the Nez Perce Indians.*